Soul Searching

Soul Searching
The Journey of Thomas Merton

Edited by Morgan C. Atkinson

with Jonathan Montaldo

LITURGICAL PRESS
Collegeville, Minnesota

www.litpress.org

Cover design by Al Moreschi Design with Ann Blattner. Front cover photos of Thomas Merton by Sybille Akers (foreground) and John Lyons (background). Used with permission of the Merton Legacy Trust and the Thomas Merton Center at Bellarmine University, Louisville, KY.

1	2	3	4	5	6	7	8	9

Library of Congress Cataloging-in-Publication Data

Soul searching : the journey of Thomas Merton / edited by Morgan Atkinson, with Jonathan Montaldo.
    p. cm.
  ISBN 978-0-8146-1873-8 (pbk.)   ISBN 978-0-8146-3264-2 (cloth)
    1. Merton, Thomas, 1915–1968. 2. Trappists—United States—Biography.
3. Monks—United States—Biography. I. Atkinson, Morgan. II. Montaldo,
Jonathan.
BX4705.M542S68 2008
271'.12502—dc22
[B]   2008030422

For Brayden, Will, and Ben:
"Mercy within mercy within mercy"

Contents

Introduction   1

    Part 1
      The Young Merton in New York   13

    Part 2
      Gethsemani   43

    Part 3
      Opening to the World   115

    Part 4
      Points West . . . and East   181

Biographies   201

Photo Credits   207

Introduction

Seeds

Thomas Merton articulated with such clarity the reality of God's presence in the world.

—Dr. Bonnie Thurston

He was studying Mahatma Gandhi and the Chinese mystics and Zen Buddhism when most people had never heard of Zen or Buddhism.

—Fr. John Dear

Merton is, in a sense, the lost soul of the twentieth century, looking for redemption, looking for recovery, looking for God.

—Sr. Kathleen Deignan

These three insights say a lot to me. In a nutshell they are why I find Thomas Merton compelling enough to devote two years to creating a documentary about him. They are why for more than thirty years I have read his work and been fascinated by his life.

For me these quotes define Merton as someone who:

1) wrote about the essence of life in a way that connects with a remarkably wide array of readers;

2) thought outside conventional "spiritual boxes" and was always looking for ways to find common ground with other spiritual traditions;

This picture of Thomas Merton has always been a favorite. It captures him in full stride—joyful, engaged, fully human. It could be called the compass for the documentary Soul Searching: The Journey of Thomas Merton, *as I referred to it often in trying to bring him to life for viewers.*

3) despite his extraordinary gifts, had an abundance of human foibles with which most of us struggle. And thankfully he wasn't too proud to admit it. In fact, it's his struggle with his humanity that makes his writing and life so interesting.

These three insights also made me think I should try to put together this book.

Another book about Thomas Merton? Since he died in 1968 there have been well over a hundred books written about Merton. These have been amplified by documentaries, plays, and all manner of magazine articles. Obviously people are interested in this man whom I feel safe in calling the twentieth century's most famous Christian monk. I doubt there is very much competition for this designation, but nevertheless, as the scholar and writer Anthony Padovano told me, "Thomas Merton is one of those figures who has achieved a kind of mythic stature. I think you achieve a mythic stature when you somehow or other symbolize and connect with very deep needs in the human psyche, and I think that Thomas Merton did that."

OK, but another book? Here's my case for this one. I'm a filmmaker and in creating the PBS documentary *Soul Searching: The Journey of Thomas Merton* I interviewed some thirty Merton friends and scholars, tracing how this complex man traveled his spiritual path. It came to more than sixty hours of interviews. These were then squeezed into a one-hour documentary. That left a lot of very rich material that didn't fit into a program designed for a visual medium. I agree with Dr. Padovano's assessment that Merton's life and writing tell us something important about ourselves and about the mysteries of the Spirit. A book including a far wider sampling of the insights from these interviews offers a great opportunity to share more about this important man and his spiritual journey. If you accept that premise, read on.

Journals—the Seedbed

Most Merton books tell the story of a twentieth-century spiritual master who after a rowdy youth spent his adult years living as a monk in a rural Kentucky monastery. Or as my father said when I first mentioned Merton some thirty years ago, "Thomas Merton? Wasn't he the guy who wrote a famous book and locked himself away for the rest of his life?"

Dad was a little off with his chronology, not to mention his understanding of Merton's life. Merton was already "locked away" when he wrote his most famous book, *The Seven Storey Mountain*. He lived as a monk of the Abbey of Gethsemani for twenty-seven years, seemingly in near total isolation but in actuality fully engaged with all corners of the world.

Merton baffled my father. As a working Hollywood writer he had to admire Merton's prodigious writing output, but as a man with Epicurean tastes he could not fathom why anyone would embrace a monastic discipline. Equally puzzling to him was why I was suddenly so interested in Merton.

His doubt was understandable. Growing up I had shown little inclination toward spiritual matters, certainly not as expressed by a Trappist monk. I grew up a Presbyterian and by my late teens had become an observant agnostic. At the time of the Merton discussion with my father I was twenty-five, a college graduate looking for a life in filmmaking but not making much headway. My parents probably told their friends I was "looking for myself." Their friends would've nodded sympathetically. Many faced the same situation with their children, late-blooming baby-boomers trying to find their stride. Now suddenly I was showing interest in a monk who had belonged to one of the most austere orders in the Roman Catholic Church, popularly known as Trappists, but formally known as the Cistercians. For my father there was consolation in the probability that Merton and monks would soon join Transcendental Meditation in my catalogue of abandoned interests.

3

Yet here it is more than thirty years later and I'm still interested in Thomas Merton. I became a Catholic because of him. I spent two years making a documentary about his life. Before that I made two other documentaries about life at the Abbey of Gethsemani. Now there's this book. What has sustained this interest and fascination? Lawrence Cunningham, the eminent Merton scholar from Notre Dame, told me, "Merton could easily be called the greatest spiritual writer, spiritual master, of the twentieth century in English-speaking America." Impressive, but my reasons are more personal. Thomas Merton's writing has quite simply been a roadmap to living my life as a more fully human being in every decade of my adult life: as a twenty-five-year-old lost in the weeds, as a thirty-four-year-old whose best friend had just died from cancer, a forty-five-year-old considering career path choices, a fifty-two-year-old on his wedding day, and now as a grandfather of three. In matters of joy, grief, or simply confusion, Merton has consistently shed light on what really matters—inspiring, teaching, entertaining, and commiserating.

My regard for Merton was such that I initially shied away from doing a documentary about him. I knew the dangers in taking on subjects that one admires a little too much. Even if objectivity could be maintained, this was Thomas Merton, an acknowledged spiritual master, an intellect well out of my depth, a life model of sorts. Besides, an excellent documentary had been made already in 1985 by Paul Wilkes.

This was and is a first-rate film. It will remain in a class by itself for its interviews of people closest to Merton's life, people whom Wilkes rightly claimed "knew him best." This wonderful documentary has qualities that will not be topped. But because of Merton's literary last will and testament, Paul Wilkes did not have access to what was then known as Merton's "restricted journals." His documentary could not consider the facts that would become apparent when these journals

Morgan Atkinson near Bear Harbor, California where Merton considered establishing a hermitage late in his life.

5

were published twenty-five years after Merton's death, beginning in 1993. These journals have now been published in seven volumes by HarperSanFranciso. They are a primary source, along with his books, letters, poetry, calligraphy, and photographs, conveying essential hints of what lies beneath the surface of Merton's public story.

Because of the recent emergence of material like the journals, I felt there was room for another Merton documentary. Merton's journals became the bedrock of my documentary. I wanted to show the truly human dimensions of this great spiritual thinker, and these journals chronicled his most private thoughts from student days until his death. The journals revealed a very human, very fallible man writing thoughts that soared but that also trudged through desolate lands of doubt and self-recrimination. Time and again one could read how Merton struggled, failed, picked himself up, and found the courage to start again. Searching . . . and finding . . . then searching for more, farther on down the road.

In the process of reading his journals, I took Merton down from any false pedestal I might have built for him. At first this was disorienting. We like our life models perfect. But in the end the journals increased my regard for Merton. By dealing so frankly with his own shortcomings, Merton challenged some of the crutches I employed in my own life. If he could face dark issues, why couldn't I? If I took what he was writing about seriously, how could I not at least try to match his courage? It seemed that, if I could tell the Merton story in a way that captured his humanity without trivializing the depth and breadth of his search, it would be worthwhile.

Soul Searching

For the name of my documentary on Merton, a friend adept in the marketing business advised putting "search" in the title. He said research shows that this active verb often leads to brisk sales. For better or worse many of us are still searching for answers. Sales considerations aside, I liked the word "search" because it also captured an essential element of Merton's life. "Restless" is another much-used description. Jonathan Montaldo, an editor of Merton's journals, confirmed to me that always stretching forward in his search for a deeper experience of God and of what it might mean to be a more complete human being was a continuing element in Merton's monastic life. Merton, he said, was never satisfied with any of society's "obligatory answers." He couldn't even swallow the easy answers he was tempted to fashion for himself. "So what looks like intellectual and emotional instability from our outside-of-his-experience perspective as readers," Montaldo said, "was really his way of finding new energies to deepen his spiritual life. If you view Merton's searching for the truth in contemplative experiences outside of Christianity, to take only one aspect of Merton's interests and studies, as instability, I feel you miss the point of Merton's life trajectory entirely. Dissatisfaction with himself and his present knowledge, and with his Western culture's 'easy answers,' was the fuel that kept his spiritual life on fire, kept him searching for God. Complacency and settling down were Merton's spiritual life's greatest enemies."

I cautioned myself, as I would often with the other voices I would listen to in conversations, that Montaldo's slant on Merton was probably a very personal reading of Merton's text. Yet there was something I could agree with in viewing Merton as someone relentlessly searching for the truth. It seemed very '60s and also very much in keeping with Joseph Campbell's description of the timeless quest of the hero. That struck a chord within me. As a child, at bedtime I had been read the Greek myths as well as the tales of King Arthur. The "searching" Merton I was now reading as an adult blended seamlessly with the Lancelot, Odysseus, and Springsteen of my youth.

Yes, Springsteen. After all, what could be more mythic than a rock star? In my estimation Bruce Springsteen was another bigger-than-life figure searching for the truth. In his signature song from the mid-1970s, "Born to Run," Springsteen declared he wanted to break loose from the conventions of a confining small town and go find "if love is real." For me that's what Merton seemed up to—making the ultimate commitment to finding the ultimate love, one that would not fail him.

Seeking a Merton Choir

My documentary on Merton was undertaken in the fall of 2004 and reluctantly completed in 2006. I say "reluctantly" because quite honestly I regretted the project ending. For two very enjoyable years I was privileged to travel around the country interviewing Merton's friends and monastic colleagues, as well as scholars of his work. From the start of my work I knew the main voice I wanted in the program was Merton's, speaking in the personal, conversational manner of his journals. I wanted to complement this with the thoughts of a mix of people who would not simply praise the good monk and great writer but would help present the complexity of this man. I wanted a variety of voices, a Merton choir.

In casting this Merton choir I traveled from coast to coast. From Manhattan skyscrapers to California redwoods, my criteria in selecting people to interview was pretty simple. Did they actually know Merton well? Had they lived in community with him? If they didn't know him firsthand, had they written a compelling book about him or about topics in which Merton was interested? Could they talk about him in a way that was accessible? Honestly, it also helped if they lived in an interesting locale.

In my travels I had the good fortune of meeting many generous people, generous and patient. As I talked with them it became clear that there were many Mertons running free. By this I mean different people had different perceptions of just who Merton was. Lawrence Cunningham at Notre Dame confirmed as much.

"What Thomas Merton are you interested in?" he asked. "Are you interested in Thomas Merton the monk? Are you interested in Thomas Merton the literary critic? Are you interested in Thomas Merton the poet? The social justice person? The person of peace? The guy who writes on spiritual theology? There are many Thomas Mertons, at least from the perspective of his writings."

He concluded by saying that Merton was really "unclassifiable." Not the best of news for a documentary producer attempting to do in some way just that.

Merton's Neighborhoods

Aside from interviewing people about Merton, I felt I needed to see where he had spent his adult life. Traveling to New York, Gethsemani, Louisville, and points west, my goal became to put myself as much as possible *in* Merton's place. While attempting to do so I kept in mind what Dom John Eudes Bamberger had told me. He had been a student of Merton's and also a good friend. As the monastery's resident psychiatrist he had worked closely with Merton in the screening of Gethsemani's candidates for community life. So he knew Merton and monastic life well. He described the frustration of many novice monks who had been drawn to monastic life at Gethsemani because of how Merton described it. Their consternation grew steadily as days, months, years went by and they were not seeing or experiencing the same revelations that Merton had and had written about, even though they were in essentially the same environment. Dom John Eudes would counsel the aspirants to consider that perhaps Merton was unusually perceptive as well as equipped with extraordinary powers of description. This says nothing about his unique spiritual gifts.

Dom John Eudes's story helped me to have no illusions about seeing *as* Merton saw, but I figured I could at least in many cases observe (and share with viewers) *what* he saw. Thanks to the hospitality of several monastic communities, I was able to live in monasteries in Kentucky, New York, the New Mexico desert, and the California redwoods. I also lived in Merton's hermitage at Gethsemani and kept his hours, sort of. My adherence to his rigorous schedule usually trailed off after the first day or two. But I did mindfully walk his Kentucky woods as well as the

New Mexico desert and the Bear Harbor seashore in California that had excited him so much.

Some have been disappointed that I confined my travels to the continental United States even though Merton was profoundly influenced by Europe and Asia (not to mention South America and the Middle East). This was due in part to a modest production budget but also because the U.S. is where Merton spent all but a few months of his adult life. The "adult Merton," from age twenty to fifty-three, is the period of life on which I chose to focus. I kept reminding myself that mine was not an attempt to create a cradle-to-grave documentary as Paul Wilkes had done. The goal was to create a human, lively portrait of Merton that might inspire viewers to explore Merton more deeply on their own.

Spare Parts

At the end of my travels I had captured some two hundred hours of footage, including the interviews. The editing of this rich material presented the only unpleasant part of the work. Trying to find the essence of Merton, I had cast an intentionally wide net. Now, unavoidably, there was so much material, very rich material, that was left unused. It was frustrating in that I knew how much these conversations meant to me. I believed they could also have meaning for anyone interested in the spiritual dimension of life, particularly for those interested in the life and times of Thomas Merton. The solution seemed to be a book that incorporates more highlights of the "Merton choir" interviews.

These interviews are far from academic lectures, as none of my conversation partners spoke from notes. They allowed me to capture them speaking unrehearsed the candid but informed insights about a man they knew and loved very well. These generous people have allowed me the unusual license to reproduce their reflections without any input into the editing of what are their conversational remarks. If you want to know best who my conversation partners are and what they most seriously and thoughtfully conclude about Merton's legacy, I urge you to follow up this introduction by reading their books and their articles.

I have organized this material by using four geographic centers of Merton's adult life as lenses through which to see him. The areas are New York City; the Abbey of Gethsemani in rural Kentucky; Louisville, Kentucky; and points west and east (to accommodate his travels in the last year of his life). To each geographic center I've assigned significant issues of Merton's life. For example, the New York section includes Merton's time at Columbia University, his "playboy" years, early writing, his brief flirtation with communism, and ultimately his conversion to Catholicism. To illuminate these issues I call on the expertise of the Merton choir, or pertinent excerpts from my interviews with these people. My hope is that you will enjoy listening with me as this panel of Merton experts weighs in.

So, let the search begin . . . or continue.

Part 1

The Young Merton in New York

New York City Serenade

New York, you are mine! I love you.

So Thomas Merton wrote as he entered the New York harbor in 1935 bound for school at Columbia University in Manhattan. Decades later, when he would return for a brief meeting with the Zen Buddhism scholar D. T. Suzuki, Merton acknowledged that he was in his heart a New Yorker. His autobiography, The Seven Storey Mountain, is in large part set in New York. He loved the vitality of the city with its diverse and energetic people. It's the city where he spent his formative college years at Columbia and where he established some of the most important and lasting friendships of his life. New York City is for Merton an important "seed" for his later contemplative life at Gethsemani. But New York is also the place where the young Merton would find everything about life "intolerable." The negativity he came to associate with Manhattan seemed to stem from a self-loathing that grew within him because of the life choices he made in New York City and earlier in England during his freshman year at Cambridge. New York, he said, "did not prove to be any good for me." Its culture became a paradigm of American culture for Merton, but more personally the city represented the consequences of a tumultuous and unstable early life. As a young monk writing his autobiography, he would rail against Manhattan and try to kick its dust from his shoes. As a mature monk, Merton would look back on the city of his youth with love.

Columbia University was like a welcoming mother for the young Merton. He arrived on campus bruised from his first year failures at Cambridge. Columbia became the closest thing to a home he had had until that time.

As I walked the Columbia campus, as I admired the beauty of Corpus Christi Church where Merton was baptized a Catholic, and as I drank coffee in Greenwich Village, I tried to conjure before my mind's eye Merton in New York. I called on my Merton choir members to describe this young man fresh off the boat from England. It's 1935, and Tom Merton is embarking on a chapter of his life that marks him indelibly and eventually makes him famous in a world for which he had great ambivalence.

∾   ∾   ∾

Paul Elie: I've come to know Robert Giroux, Merton's editor and initially his classmate at Columbia. When he recalls Thomas Merton at Columbia, he recalls a young man of frenzied activity who literally couldn't sit still. Such was the appeal of the clubs, the classes, the newspapers, the dining out, the excursions downtown that Columbia offered. He just did not rest. Merton himself would say later that this restlessness was theological, that he didn't have a sense of his true orientation and so was casting around in all directions. To put it a little more prosaically, and this is what Robert Giroux told me, his life lacked an order that would give him a little peace.

Monica Weis: I think of Merton in that time as the man about town. He was discovering friendship and had wonderful friendships with people like the artist Ad Reinhardt and the poet Bob Lax. Being part of the Columbia journalism project there, the *Jester*, he spent time with those guys. He hung out with them and discovered questions that they were interested in. I think the intellectual discussions late at night must have been extremely stimulating. Here was a place for him to discover, I'll say "home" in quotation marks, because this is a man who was always searching for "home."

Going to the jazz clubs, I think that really reflects something of the personality of Merton. Jazz is an improv kind of music but it has rules.

16

He loved improvisation but then discovered that there are principles and rules of life. So jazz could be a very good metaphor for him during his student days at Columbia.

Elena Malits: As a young person, when he was going to what we would call high school in England, he was already interested in jazz. And that certainly continued in his days at Cambridge and then after he came to Columbia. I think that's a very good metaphor for Merton's life because jazz is a very complex kind of music. It has a certain kind of gait and rhythm. It is intricate in the arrangements of notes. It's the kind of music, I think, if you get interested in it at all, it hooks you. And that's the kind of personality Thomas Merton had.

John Eudes Bamberger: I think anyone who knew Merton for any length of time quickly saw that he did everything with full speed ahead. He was a type that once he jumped on something, he landed with both feet. That would get him in trouble when he was younger, and it would occasionally get him in trouble later on in the monastery when he would write certain things. I remember him telling me once, "I'm going to get hit over the head for this, but I'm going to say it anyhow." There was always a certain spontaneity about Merton that made one feel that he was always right there with you.

Christine Bochen: I had the experience of meeting a woman who was also a student at Columbia when Merton was there, and what she remembered was that he always had a group of people around him, and I think that captures something of the Merton that we've come to know. The one who is the solitary also had, in this place, both a hunger and a capacity for human relationships. She remembers walking into the student union and seeing Merton surrounded by people.

Michael Mott: When I talked to a friend from Merton's Columbia days, Jinny Burton, about him, she gave rather a telling remark that the two of them were dance partners. She said Merton was almost a professional dancer. He was terrific, but she remarked that he couldn't forget

himself. You know, you're a dancer, you've got to forget your body and do all kinds of things, but he was too self-aware, just too self-aware, she said. I thought that was interesting.

Elena Malits: I did some graduate study at Union Theological Seminary, which is right across from Columbia where Merton was an undergraduate. So I used to eat in some of the places he talked about, on the Upper West Side. I used to look at Columbia students and say to myself, "Which of these young people I'm looking at now would Thomas Merton be like?" The thing that strikes me about him is that he was intellectually curious beyond belief. He read everything he could get his hands on. I think that he thought anything in print was worthy of at least starting. If it wasn't any good he would toss it aside. But he had almost an insatiable literary interest. He was interested in politics, in social issues. I can't think of anything that was going on in the United States in the mid-1930s when he was at Columbia that would not have been of great concern to him. He had a wonderful sense of humor; everybody who knows him says that. They say he was fun to be around. He belonged to the people who were probably the most interesting set in his class. As somebody who has taught in college all her life, there are just some classes of students that come around that are just more interesting than others. In 1935, when he came to Columbia, he got in with a group of bright young men who wanted to conquer the world, to know everything there was to know. I think his friendships were absolutely crucial to the person he later became.

Cambridge

I've always enjoyed descriptions of the young Merton. They are what first allowed me to make a connection with him. Though my own

This is another favorite Merton photo. Actually it's an outtake from his freshman year class picture at Clare College, Cambridge. Everyone looks pretty much on the same page with the exception of Merton, whose mind is definitely someplace else. It seems to aptly sum up that wayward freshman year.

school days had little of the scholastic seriousness of Merton's, I can nonetheless relate to his life on a college campus. I've noticed that Merton's youthful experiences seem to attract many other readers, perhaps for some of the same reasons as my own. Here is a towering spiritual figure who did not emerge fully formed from a cradle of piety. His advocacy of a spiritual life had credibility because he knew whereof he spoke in describing the limitations of a world based on purely material aspirations.

For my film Soul Searching *I wanted to convey just how enthusiastically and fully the young Thomas Merton had "embraced the world." This was no recluse holed up in his dorm room. He danced every dance with gusto. If a spiritual path could be rooted in such earthy ground, then that was encouraging for those of us far outside the cloister.*

As Merton describes these New York days in The Seven Storey Mountain, *the vitality comes crackling off the page but so does his angst. Robert Giroux, Merton's friend and editor, noted that Merton's energy was almost manic. It was as if he was trying to obliterate something gnawing within him. Anthony Padovano observed to me that, in researching his biography of Merton, he sensed many of the ingredients of a nervous breakdown in the young student. What prompted all this?*

Jonathan Montaldo: Certainly his experience at Cambridge University, before coming to New York—in his autobiography Cambridge becomes the "pit of hell"—must have affected Merton for the rest of his life. There's no reason why Cambridge in and of itself is hell, but for Merton it was hell. He had made it hell. He did not make good grades and was in danger of losing his scholarship. He fooled around and is reported to have made a young woman pregnant. And somehow he gets out of that situation. His mother's father's money funneled through Tom Bennett, a London-based friend of Merton's deceased father, Owen, might have bought Tom Merton out of the trouble.

It's Tom Bennett who tells Merton, "You're finished at Cambridge. You have to go back to America." Certainly that affected him, probably for the rest of his life. It probably explains his guilt, that is, his uneasiness with himself, his sinfulness, his selfishness which he reports in *The Seven Storey Mountain*.

William Shannon: At Cambridge Merton not only had lost his faith, he really lost any sense of direction in his life. He didn't give the time to his studies that he should have. He did a lot of drinking. I think that was one of the temptations of his life always. I think that he could have very easily become an alcoholic if he hadn't been more careful about it. He once said, "I love beer and therefore I love the world." But he also loved bourbon.

There's an interesting story in one of the novels that the young Merton wrote called *The Labyrinth*, in which he tells of a party that took place at Clare College at Cambridge University. The story appears in a chapter of the novel called "The Party in the Night." Naomi Burton Stone, Merton's literary agent, who read the original copy, recalled that there was a mock crucifixion that took place at that party and she wondered whether the event was autobiographical and if Merton was the one who had been "crucified." Interestingly, when he filled out his naturalization papers as an American citizen, one of the identifying marks was a scar in the palm of his hand.

Michael Mott: I don't deny the possibility that Merton got a woman with child while he was at Cambridge. He may or may not have. Doing research for my biography of Merton, I was amused when his good friend Robert Lax told me that when he first heard about Merton, the rumor around Columbia was that he had fathered at least two children in Cambridge! It's a hell of a lot more glamorous on college campuses, I believe, to arrive as the putative father of two illegitimate children than it is to come as a flunky from your grades, which is the reason he was at Columbia rather than Cambridge.

"I don't know" is the short answer to the question of whether Merton got a young woman pregnant. I suspect that there was some scandal because there's a letter, a much later letter, in which he's writing to his former guardian Tom Izod Bennett, in which he says, "If you're still in touch with that woman, please let me know." So presumably a woman existed. In his book about Merton his friend Ed Rice speculates, from a story he heard from Merton, that the mother and the child were killed during the Blitz in the Second World War. But I think that this was a child of Merton's imagination.

Now, if he did indeed father a child, she would have been a woman of a different class to him, this is obvious. The drill, I'm afraid, was that you paid lawyers to pay her off. Everybody would have then agreed that he would have no recourse to her at all. She would have no recourse to him, except through the lawyers, and they were there to prevent that. It is possible that there was such an arrangement. Now, abortion was illegal in England at that time and for long after, but it was not unknown. Whether there was a live birth, I doubt. I can't, you know, go any further than that. I did my attempted researches, but that's not an easy thing to check up on, especially, you know, if for forty or fifty years people have been wiping that information out.

Writing

Some of these insights surprised me and admittedly tend toward the sensational. I wondered if including them had value or would be merely titillating. I did not want Soul Searching *to come across as a paparazzi version of Thomas Merton. In trying to decide what seemed fair game to include, I considered how Merton himself dealt with the issue. From everything I have heard or read he despised fakery, almost always opting for what was honest and authentic despite the consequences.*

In writing his private journals Merton could have airbrushed any flaws. He didn't. My guess is that he felt it was important to share the human dimensions and struggles of his spiritual life. As Anthony Padovano said, "He writes in his journals about his pettiness, his envy, his sexual temptations, his doubts. He wanted everyone to know that the mystical journey was profoundly human. That it wasn't exotic. It wasn't artificial."

Merton told the truth of his life as best he could, without hiding or sensationalizing. That was the approach and balance I sought to achieve in my film. Besides, these weren't exactly Fleet Street scandalmongers telling these stories to me. If they felt it was appropriate to relate this information, I was at peace in sharing it with a wider audience. Admitting his humanity was one of Merton's most generous gifts to his readers.

Lawrence Cunningham suggested to me that another of Merton's gifts was writing about his spiritual turmoil in a way that was accessible and not overly pietistic. I agree heartily. Merton was the first spiritual writer whose thoughts weren't simply white noise for me. Many of the Merton choir are themselves writers of spiritual literature. I wanted to get their take on Merton's writing as it began to develop.

Michael Mott: I think Merton finds a way of responding to the hunger for religion and religious life, the hunger for God that can be put in terms that are not off-putting, that are on-putting, if that can be used as a word, so that you finish reading it and you say, "I'm not sure about that yet, but this man is really speaking my language. And he's speaking my language about subjects that very few other people are speaking about coherently, at my level, at my mental level. This man is interested in what I am thinking. He is interested in my search for God and he's helping me in that search."

We used to talk about "sending in clear." When you send in clear, the message is received. If you try and muddle it, or get pretentious, you scramble a message. Here's a good old army story about that. We're sitting in the trenches and we send a message back by runner and the message leaves us: "Send in reinforcements, we're going to advance." And it gets back to brigade headquarters as "Send three and four pence, we going to a dance." This very seldom happened with Merton; he "sent in clear," very clear.

I think Merton always considered himself extraordinary. I have the feeling that he earned that idea when he was about three months old or maybe younger, when his mother watched him with such passion the whole time, and everything he did was important. She impressed upon him that everything he did was important, and so important that she wrote it all down in a book called *Tom's Book*. All of that ended when his brother John Paul arrived when Tom was three. His mother then started a journal for John Paul. I think that was a big crisis and he spent the rest of his life filling in *Tom's Book*, which his mother had abandoned.

Elena Malits: I think it's impossible to think about Thomas Merton without paying attention to the importance of writing in his life. I personally believe that writing was as essential to Merton as breathing. When he was eleven years old in France, he talks about hanging out with a group of boys who would walk around with their hands in their back pockets seriously talking about the novels they were writing. This is at age eleven! I think writing was an absolutely central mode of communication. Merton spoke well, but I think writing gave him the kind of distance that speaking doesn't give anyone. Speaking gives you immediacy. Writing gives you the chance to step back a little bit from your audience and choose more carefully what you want to say. I think personally that Merton was a compulsive writer. He had to discipline himself not to write, the way alcoholics have to distance themselves from the nearest bottle.

Jonathan Montaldo: We know for certain that Merton was writing short stories when he was a young kid. We also know, and I think importantly, that at least at the age of sixteen he was writing journals. Now those early journals don't exist, as far as we know now. He says in his extant journals that he destroyed them. But from sixteen on he is writing journals. Merton at Columbia is also writing novels and trying to get them published.

He writes in his autobiography and in his early journals about outings to a cottage in Olean, New York, that was owned by the brother-in-law of his best friend Robert Lax. It's on the river. The guys and girlfriends go there one summer to write novels. It's a pretty big cottage. It has a very large living room with a fireplace. It has three or four bedrooms off of this big room. It has a very huge porch. I had always thought, before I saw it for myself, it was a small cottage with all these young people packed in there like the poor, but it wasn't. It's rather comfortable actually.

I met one of Robert Lax's nephews who was actually at the cottage, as an eleven-year-old boy while Ed Rice, Bob Gerdy, Tom Merton, and Lax were hanging out during the summer. He told me that Rice and Gerdy were really kind of men's men. They were building tree houses. They were always doing physical things. Merton he remembers was very, very quiet. Very much to himself, always writing. So this belies the image of Merton as a kind of a wild guy. He probably had many sides to him. He was the guy who liked to go out and drink and swagger after dames, and then he was this very serious person that perhaps he often didn't share with all of his friends.

Catholicism

Merton's writing life in New York produced unpublished novels, poems, and, as always, journal entries. All reveal a young man whose life seemed on a collision course with crisis. To be fair to him, a state of turmoil really isn't too surprising for people at the end of their time in college. Very significant decisions often have to be made. Throw in an ongoing Depression, a pending war, and the stakes are heightened. Factor within these historical contexts Merton's typical intensity, marked by bouts with nervous exhaustion, and you've got quite a stew. Consider also that Merton's vocational aspirations had changed in a few years from the diplomatic corps to journalism to teaching. Now suddenly he was looking at a spiritual life seriously.

∾   ∾   ∾

Elena Malits: I think to really understand Thomas Merton's interest in Catholicism, you have to go back to the time when he's sixteen years old and spends time in Rome on his own. I've always been fascinated with this, and I do not take it lightly, that I think Merton's first real attraction to the Catholic Church was through art.

He found himself going around to the smaller churches in Rome, the churches that do not draw huge crowds but have interesting mosaics. He talks about the image of Christ that he met in the Byzantine mosaics. The "strong Christ," as he says, of the apocalypse, of the martyrs. He says that while he went to see the art, without understanding what was happening, he found something else happening to him that went beyond the art. He just liked to go to those places and sit and be quiet.

Merton goes from visiting these churches to later reflect, when he's back in his room at a *pensione*, that he suddenly and really is in touch with his father who had just recently died. I think that whole sequence of events around that time in Rome was extremely important, and he tries to act on it. He buys himself a New Testament, and he sets up some rules for himself, and then he goes back and starts college at Cambridge and like any other college freshman suddenly he's overwhelmed by all the new things and excitement around him. I don't think he forgets about it. I think it just recedes into his unconscious.

I've tried to look at the conversion stories of many people, and often there is an earlier experience that compels somebody and then recedes. But at another time, when something else happens, that is the deep source, the deep well that the person can draw on.

Monica Weis: I don't think Merton was coming apart in New York City. I think he was trying to get it together. I really trace some of his "getting it together" back to his trip to Rome, when he was looking at all of the art in old, ancient, classical Rome and then wandered into some churches and was captured by the mosaics in there. He says in his autobiography that these were his first lessons, his first instructions in Christianity. I've been to the church of Ss. Cosmas and Damien to look at that mosaic. He was startled by the blue that's in there. And it is quite amazing.

One time when I was in Rome I did a little Merton pilgrimage of my own to some of his favorite churches. I wanted to know why, after he had had the vision of his father in his bedroom in Rome, he ran across town to the church of Santa Sabina, which is not nearby, and went into that church to kneel at the altar rail and say the Our Father, which he hadn't said since he was about three years old. When I walked into the church I think I knew the reason why. It's the light. I think that place may have triggered something in his mind about memories of Prades, France, where he was born, and the light that was part of his early childhood and the light in southern France when he and his father Owen lived together in the town of St. Antonin.

I now know why painters go to southern France to work, because the light there is something I've never seen before. There's something about Santa Sabina and its light. Now maybe that's why he had to go there. I don't think he would be conscious of it and say that, but perhaps that can be something of the seed or the driving force that was continuing to bear some fruit in his time at Columbia. He's looking and saying to himself, "Where is the light? Where can the light be for me?"

And "the light" happens intellectually as he's reading Etienne Gilson and Aldous Huxley. It happens spiritually when he's reading the life of the Jesuit poet Gerard Manley Hopkins. He realizes that Hopkins made a spontaneous decision to become a Catholic and, as he writes in *The Seven Storey Mountain*, "Why can't I do the same?" And he runs down the street to find someone at Corpus Christi Church. I think that's all part of a piece that we're only now beginning to understand as we look back at Merton's life and begin to see how maybe prophetic some of these experiences have been in drawing him on to a deeper sense of himself and a deeper sense of finding God in himself and finding himself in God.

Christine Bochen: In *The Seven Storey Mountain*, when Merton is reflecting on his conversion, he talks about how God brought him and this group of friends together at Columbia. For Merton, the path to conversion is a very sacramental path, and what I mean by that is that he comes to experience God through the things of this world, and through the people of this world. So in some way, in all of that fun and all of that intellectual vigor and excitement, there was also for Merton the moment of awakening of the spirit.

Lawrence Cunningham: I think Merton was very typical of the age in which he lived. That is, this was a young man, obviously a budding intellectual, who had been deeply touched by what I call the modernist canon in literature. He's reading the people at this time who are revolutionizing studies in English and American Literature, people like William Blake and John Donne, like Gerard Manley Hopkins, T. S. Eliot and W. H. Auden. These are writers, especially twentieth-century writers like James Joyce, who had a very deep sense of the crisis of Western civilization, the loss of values, the disappointment that occurred after the slaughtering war in 1918, the First World War, and who were seeking some kind of framework within which to live.

Merton himself was in New York during the time of the Depression, so there was also this huge discussion about social justice and equity. He himself flirted with, for a very short period of time, the Communist Party. I think it was Lyndon Johnson who said that nobody who was really thinking in the 1930s was unaffected by the attraction of communism after the crisis of the Depression in 1929.

The bapistry at Corpus Christi Church.

Sometime after the Second World War there was a famous collection of short essays written under the generic title *The God that Failed*. These were basically stories about people who had wholeheartedly embraced Marxism. Many of them who had joined the Communist Party felt that god with a small *g* had failed. As a consequence, a lot of them had become Catholic. But, just to back up a second, Merton's first interest in Catholicism came, interestingly enough, because of his interest in literature. He had read Dante, who is saturated with Catholic ideas. When he became interested in the poetry of Gerard Manley Hopkins, he began to read in the background of Catholic intellectual thought.

There's a famous scene in *The Seven Storey Mountain* where he talks about buying this book that he saw in a window of Scribner's Bookstore by the great French thinker Etienne Gilson called *The Spirit of Medieval Philosophy*. Merton says that when he read that book it changed his life. Gilson wrote that in the Middle Ages the notion of God articulated by Thomas Aquinas and others was that God was the source of all being, and was the only subsistent being, and that all other being participates in God's being. Merton writes, "For the first time in my life I began to realize everything was interconnected." That led him then to begin to read other Catholic writers.

Let me add one other point. Merton is reading this book of Gilson's precisely at the time when there was a great renaissance occurring in Catholic letters and Catholic philosophy. This is the period of Jacques Maritain, the great philosopher, and of his wife Raissa, who would later become friends of Thomas Merton. This was the period when Dorothy Day had become a Catholic and was associated with Peter Maurin and the Catholic Worker movement. This was the time when new thinking about art was being generated by British artists like Eric Gill. This was a time when many people had lost faith in communism and were attracted to Catholicism. Some people cynically said they gave up one absolute worldview for another absolute worldview, but there was a kind of a flowering moment, people have called it the "Catholic renaissance," in that precise period of Merton's budding interest in Catholicism.

I do think that Merton was a searcher, and he first searched in literature. I think that Catholicism attracted him first of all intellectually, reading Gilson and others. Then he was interested in the aesthetics of Catholicism. There's another scene in *The Seven Storey Mountain* where he mentions walking into Corpus Christi Church one day, and he was overcome by the fact that there were ordinary people there in the middle of the day just praying. That struck him very forcefully. When he made a trip to Cuba, while he was a graduate student, he had a kind of religious experience going into a church, when he heard a whole group of school children with this Franciscan cry out, "*Yo Creo,*" I believe, as they began reciting The Apostles Creed. I think Merton saw some organic wholesomeness in Catholicism which was very attractive to him.

Communism

It has been pointed out by astute observers like Lawrence Cunningham and Anthony Padovano that a conversion is an ongoing process. For my film, I wanted to try to show Merton's conversion to Catholicism through his experiences in New York City unfolding step by step. I thought an initial stage in Merton's conversion was an attraction to communism. To my surprise, some of my conversation partners were reluctant to talk about Merton's passing interest in communism while at Columbia. Apparently being "Red" still carries menace almost twenty years after the collapse of the Soviet Union. They felt that Merton's legacy was already under enough fire in the institutional church and his critics didn't need any more ammunition. I countered that a consideration of communism served as a critical step in Merton's spiritual development. It had resonance for me because of a parallel in my own life. In my senior year in high school I carried a copy of Chairman Mao's Little Red Book *conspicuously placed atop my other school books. It was an edgy bumper sticker of sorts that announced my seriousness . . . about something, I wasn't quite sure what. After several weeks no one had noticed, probably a good thing in that I hadn't read beyond the first chapter. I put the book away.*

Merton's consideration of communism was more deeply felt than mine, and I thought it should be explored.

Jonathan Montaldo: I think Merton's attraction to communism was superficial. He was recruited. He said he went to one meeting of a communist cell. He took an alias of Frank Swift, but he only went to one meeting, and then his interest dropped. We don't hear any more about it. I think Merton was much more interested in his interior life, even at that stage of his life. Maybe his attraction to communism was that everyone else was doing it. He does not make, in my memory of reading *The Seven Storey Mountain*, a big pitch for communism, its correctness, or for the Communist Party. It is part of his story, but I feel a small part.

Elena Malits: In *The Seven Storey Mountain* Merton talks about how everybody in the early 1930s at Columbia was talking about the importance of what the communists were saying. The word "Pinko" was thrown around very lightly. Merton was the kind of person that would never just write off words that were used to describe a movement or group of people who were making themselves known. I think that Thomas Merton understood that there was something essentially good in Marxism that led people to be critical, in the best sense of the term, of society. That's what attracted him. I don't think Merton was ever really attracted to the Russian brand of communism. He was interested in studying Marx, and that's quite a different thing. In *The Seven Storey Mountain* I've always thought that Merton himself jokes about his interest in communism. I think he does not do himself justice: like many young people he got attracted to communism because of his idealism and the kind of people he met. There's a passage in *The Seven Storey Mountain* where he talks about his great discussion on communism in the apartment on Park Avenue of a young woman as they looked out the window and drank their various drinks. He makes fun of this as how superficial his interest in communism was. Well, I think you can take it that way and, given this is a young monk looking back on his college life, you can understand that. But I really believe that he understood why serious intellectuals in America in the 1930s were dissatisfied. This is the time of the Great Depression and a lot of people didn't have any idea what might be done. They thought Marxism offered a solution. I think that's the ground of his interest in communism.

Paul Elie: In *The Seven Storey Mountain* Merton makes a lot out of his attraction to communism. I think he overstates it a little. What he's getting at is the appeal of communism as an idea and a way of life that he'd taken from books and hoped to find lived out in the world around him. Well, as he tells it in the book, the grand ideals of communism weren't matched by the pretty boring meetings that he went to at Columbia, the meetings of Young Communists. Now a few years later when he went to the Trappist monastery of Gethsemani, he had a very different experience. He had read about monks and monasticism in lots of books, particularly a long entry in the *Catholic Encyclopedia* describing the Trappists. So he went down to the Trappist monastery, and there it was. The monks were doing the things that they were said to do in the encyclopedia, and in works of medieval literature. It was fully happening. It wasn't a shadow of the real thing. I think he was just blown away by the correspondence between what he'd read and what he saw and felt.

Conversion

I grew up in an area of Louisville, Kentucky, where there were a lot of Catholics. We had dozens of kids in my neighborhood and most of them were Catholic. We didn't talk much about religion and my notions

33

about Catholicism were pretty sketchy. If I had any interest, it was because it seemed so very different from my Presbyterian Sunday School.

The mystery and exotic nature of this faith was summed up for me by a trip to the neighborhood Catholic church. One of my buddies took me inside and told me to wait for him. He was going to confession, which for reasons I couldn't understand he seemed to be dreading. I looked around a bit fearful myself, not sure if I was even allowed in. The array of statues and candles were different but not all that exciting to me. Then the crucified Jesus in agony caught my eye. It was definitely a departure from the smiling, handsome, hale-savior-well-met I was used to seeing in my own church. I was trying to get a sense of what that was all about when my attention was jerked upward to a large eye located in the middle of the church's high-domed ceiling. The impact that big eye had on me was literally stunning. I stared transfixed. Seconds passed, maybe minutes. I began to get dizzy and lose my orientation, but then I realized it was because I had been staring straight up for too long. I left the church a bit wobbly and with a full plate of new notions to chew on.

For several nights I lay awake mulling over the possibilities of this Catholic God. Here was a Being that was certainly very present and obviously interested in what people were doing. Over the months I'd ask the occasional question of my buddies who went to church there. They'd grown up with the eye and weren't nearly as impressed with it as I was. They did say that on what they called Holy Days the eye was lit by a bulb from within. I'd like to have seen that but not enough to go back. I was nine or ten at the time.

As I got older I didn't think too much about the eye or much else in the world of organized religion. I know for certain that reading about someone converting to Catholicism or any other spiritual path was of no interest to me. All religions, East and West, seemed so compromised by institutional bureaucracy and human foibles that none seemed even remotely credible or relevant. So as I read The Seven Storey Mountain *and began to identify with the "wild" Merton, his abrupt switch to an enthu-*

siastic embrace of all things Catholic confused and frankly repelled me. But at the same time I was also impressed by his ardor and the way he expressed it. A more apt word than "impressed" would be "envious." Merton made the spiritual life, something that had always seemed so artificial to me, sound vital, incredibly alive, and frankly the only thing in life worth being concerned about. He wrote about it with a passion I had previously found only in Rolling Stone record reviews or in a Ramparts political essay. Tom Merton wrote about the spiritual life with the intensity and color of Tom Wolfe writing about 1960s culture.

જે જે જે

Colman McCarthy: Well, I think the conversion story is what people find intriguing about Merton. Here was this intellectual hedonist, kind of a good liver, a drinker, a bit of a womanizer, and suddenly he goes to the other extreme. That fascinates people. How did that happen? Why did it happen? And when Merton explained it all, then he became a kind of mythical figure, and people are attracted to myths.

The hero is somehow doing something extraordinary which I couldn't do, and we love to get the inside story. That's what great investigative journalism is and Merton in a sense became one of those types of reporters. He was an investigative reporter going into the inner workings of the soul, and that's what his main appeal was as a writer. And he was authentic because he was living it, and so, when he had that perfect match of doing it as well as saying it, that's almost unbeatable, and that's how he became well known. And he wrote with a great flow of prose with metaphorical language, and so he became a man who attracted people and that was very compelling, because we're always searching for heroes, and so he fulfilled that need.

Lawrence Cunningham: I'd like to go back to the notion of conversion as it appears in the New Testament. The Greek word for conversion is

44

Baptism

No.	NAME OF PERSON BAPTIZED	DATE AND PLACE OF BIRTH	DATE OF BAPTISM	FATHER'S NAME MOTHER'S MAIDEN N...
108	Merton Thomas	Jan. 31, 1915 Prades, France	Nov. 16 1938	Owen Ruth Jenkins

Register

SPONSORS	PRIEST	DATE OF CONFIRMATION	Record of Marriage, Religious Profession or Sub-Diaconate. REMARKS.
Edward Rice	J. P. Moore		Conditional Baptism Convert. Effing Solemn vow. Trap Solemn Vows - Mch 19th 1947 at Gethsemane - Kentucky - Cistercian

metanoia. Now we tend to think of conversion as kind of a Saint-Paul-on-the-road-to-Damascus experience, where all of a sudden someone gets thrown from their horse, gets up and goes down the sawdust trail and confesses their change of faith. I think it's deeper and it's more subtle than that.

I think in Merton's life it's very hard to pinpoint the moment when he's a believer as opposed to a nonbeliever. But conversion literally means to turn around or to turn over, so that in every conversion there is equally an aversion. That is, by turning to something you have to turn away from something else. I think that religious conversion happens when a person leaves off a certain way of being and seeing and thinking and embraces a new way of thinking and seeing and acting. I think that happens to Merton.

He goes from a position of not really being able to pray to one who becomes a person of prayer. He thinks that many of the problems that were in his past are problems that he needs to shuck off. He wants to find a deeper meaning in his life. He wants it to be focused and so on. So there is that kind of dialectic between turning away from one way of being to turning to another way of being.

The great philosopher of religion and psychologist of religion, William James, in his book *Varieties of Religious Experience*, talks about people who are "twice born." Some people are naturally Christian or are raised in Christian homes, and then after a certain period in their life, they actually go through a different conversion. They learn a greater depth of their Christian being. I think that you can trace in Thomas Merton not a conversion but a whole series of conversions in his life.

Robert Inchausti: When Merton converted to Christianity and Catholicism, the primary conversion was a kind of heart conversion. Merton writes and speaks from the heart. But he was also an intellectual. He

Corpus Christi's baptism register for Thomas Merton.

had read James Joyce and he had read all the contemporary modernists and he hadn't made the final connection between the head and the heart. The head was still a skeptic, was still an intellectual, was sort of a Joycean culture critic until he read Etienne Gilson's book on medieval scholasticism.

In that book Gilson says, "God is not a being, God is being." Now this opened his mind because suddenly, if the medieval theologians thought of God not as a being but as being, that meant that the most powerful theologians never thought of God as a man with a long beard or any of these superstitious, sort of silly conceptions of God. The medieval theologians were as hip as any contemporary existentialist and as profound as Martin Heidegger's fundamental ontology, only three hundred years before them. And this made Merton think, "My God, there's an intellectual side to this, too, that isn't just my heartfelt acknowledgement of God. But God is not a being that one argues for or against. God is a reality that lives within, and it transcends our conception of God."

Part of Merton's problem with God, and part of our problem, too, was that his conception of God was not big enough. So it was sort of like for him, "God is greater than I thought. I was struggling with a false conception of who I thought God was, and now here I read this medieval theologian, Saint Thomas Aquinas, writing hundreds of years before my time that God is 'being' itself. God transcends my capacity to merely think about God." That was a real mind opener to him, and once he entertained the possibility that it was his conception of God that was narrow, it opened in him the desire to explore further. He started reading all the theologians, the medieval theologians, the contemporary theologians, with new interest. These weren't abstract, scholastic arguments, but they were actually talking about ideas that had contemporary significance for him. God is not something that adds on to reality to explain it. God is reality. That's what Merton learned from the medieval theologians, and that just opened the door for him, because now his head and his heart were no longer struggling and he was able to write and think within that paradigm.

William Shannon: What goes on in a person who goes through an experience of conversion? Probably many things, and they are probably very different for each person. Conversion is not simply changing from bad habits to good habits. Conversion is really achieving a whole new level of consciousness where one in a deep conversion experience comes to realize God as the hidden ground of love, which is a term that Merton used. In finding a "hidden ground of Love," Merton found God, he found his own identity, he found his communion with other people.

Christine Bochen: I've come to see that there are very few 180-degree turns in Merton's life. I would be inclined to look for the continuity in Merton's experiences. So, for example, when people think of his conversion and think of this young man living an exciting life, first at Cambridge then at Columbia, they might be shocked to find him drawn to the Catholic Church. Yet, one finds in *The Seven Storey Mountain* moments where Merton points to the awakening of the spirit which flowers in a significant way in New York when he finds his way to Corpus Christi, when he decides to take instruction, and finally when he becomes a convert. This process of conversion is interesting because it involves a turning away in one sense, a turning around, but also involves a sense of being drawn. Merton's responding to something. He says that God placed certain experiences in his path and this is not a God who for Merton is like a puppet master in the sky, but a God who is to be experienced through and in this world.

Merton came to see that at Columbia. A curiosity drew him toward experiencing God in the world. Catholicism was intellectually exciting to him, but he was moved, too, in New York and also during his visit to Cuba, by the faith of ordinary people. There was community to be found in the Catholic Church, and I think that that appealed to Merton.

John Eudes Bamberger: He had suffered a great deal actually in his earlier years before he was converted, and what he suffered most from, I believe, was the feeling of not belonging, of not being in touch with what he felt was most real. When he was converted, that was his insight, that "This is real! This is what truth is! This is what life should be about!" So he could honestly and with great energy give himself totally to it.

Anthony Padovano: What happens in a conversion is difficult to say because I think it is different for all of us. Certainly there are some elements that we could sort out. One is that it is usually an experience of enlightenment in which you see—that's why enlightenment is a good word—everything differently. Sometimes that's all of a sudden, as it seems to have been with St. Paul, or even with Augustine. Other times it seems to be much more gradual and cumulative, which is how I think it happened with Merton.

A lot of things kept moving him in a direction that helped him constantly see things differently. So that idea of a gradual enlightenment is very important. For a reason you never know, you have this "Aha, Eureka!" and nothing looks the same again. I guess the closest that most people get to it is love. When you are in love with someone, the whole world looks different all of a sudden. You look different to yourself. This other person whom you thought you didn't love looks different. Everything is different.

So enlightenment is one element in the conversion, but a second thing that comes about—and it is there from Paul to Augustine to Newman to Merton and so on—is that enlightenment summons you to a task and to take up a burden. Something must be done. Love is not only a joy but also a burden, a responsibility. "Now that I've seen the world differently, what do I do about myself and about all those things in my life that made me look at the world differently?" So the second element, Merton's burden so to speak, his need to respond responsibly to what he had seen, was eventually the Cistercian monastery at Gethsemani.

Then I guess the third element is that, as one goes about the task, one tries to connect with other people. "I'm in love, I want to tell you about that." No one is in love and says nothing. "I've had an experience and I want to let you know about that. I want to talk about that."

So there is a need to communicate, which is why so many powerful conversions lead to powerful writing, whether that's Paul or Augustine or Newman or Merton or many others.

Jonathan Montaldo: At the urging of his friend Daniel Walsh, a former professor of his at Columbia, Merton makes a Holy Week retreat in April, 1941, at the Abbey of Gethsemani. What he finds at Gethsemani turns his life around. He writes in the journal he was keeping, "I should tear out all the pages of the journals I've been writing and begin again. This is the only real city in America. Now I know that the prayers of these monks are what is holding the world together." It's hyperbole, of course, but it's a great "Aha" experience.

When Merton returns to Saint Bonaventure College in Olean, New York, where he is teaching English, he begins a somewhat anguished discernment of his future. Finally he decides that he wants more than anything to become a monk of Gethsemani. He speaks to one of the Franciscan friars who tells him to go down to the monastery, just show up, and try to get in. Merton arrives at Gethsemani's gate on December 10, 1941. He stays in the guest house three days and begins a period of formal training for the monastery on Saint Lucy's Day, December 13.

Merton wanted to be a published novelist and poet, but I don't think Merton was really tempted to do social work or become what might be called a social activist before he entered Gethsemani. He was a young man desperately seeking God, desperately seeking a meaning for his life. He wrote in his book *Love and Living* that he was so active and distracted at Columbia and in search of so many experiences that he didn't have time to really think and find out who he truly was.

At Gethsemani his life would acquire stability. He wrote that he could finally "stop arguing with the seven guys who argue inside my head and be completely quiet in front of the Face of Peace." He writes this in a truly beautiful letter to his best friend Bob Lax dated December 6, 1941, just four days before he would enter Gethsemani. He writes to Lax that "finally it's time for me to go to the Trappists and try to get in.

It's time for me to get out of the subway and out of the room full of smoke and sleep in a clean bedroom." He says, "If you have a choice between being in a novel by John O'Hara or a book by St. Teresa of Avila, I guess you've got to make the choice and don't look at these two realities as being even comparable." And then he says that while he's praying in Gethsemani's big church, everyone he loves will be praying there with him: "Lax, Gibney and Rice, my mother and father who died, and my uncle and aunt, my brother, and Bramachari and the whole mystical body of Christ, all times, all peoples, all mysteries, all miracles." So four days before he arrives at Gethsemani, now twenty-six years old, Merton already has this sense that he is going into solitude at Gethsemani bringing everyone he loved with him in the pocket of his heart, that somehow they are all going to be with him at Gethsemani. Merton is not losing everything and everyone by entering Gethsemani. He is conserving everything. He's gaining everything by going there. I think, if he had stayed in Manhattan, he would've lost everything, perhaps himself, perhaps his soul. Fear of losing his soul led him out of Manhattan to teach at Saint Bonaventure's in Olean, New York. Saint Bonaventure's was Merton's halfway house toward his monastic vocation. On that Holy Week retreat at Gethsemani in April, Merton was ready to be tipped. In December, arriving at Gethsemani's gate, he fell all the way over, flat on his face in prayer, perhaps for the first time in his life secure that he could find out who he truly was as he became a man on a path to becoming a monk.

Part 2

Gethsemani

The Promised Land

The four walls of my new freedom.

S o *Thomas Merton described his new life at the Abbey of Gethse-mani. Though my home was only an hour from the abbey, I was not aware it existed until I read* The Seven Storey Mountain *when I was twenty-five. Friends who had gone to Catholic schools had almost all made visits with parish or school groups much earlier in their lives. In the pecking order of Catholic spirituality in the 1950s and '60s, a Trappist monastery was near the top. My wife tells the story of her class field trip to what she remembers as a very austere and intimidating place. As the eighth graders from Our Lady of Lourdes explored the grounds, they came to a sign forbidding females from going any farther. Not only forbidding but threatening any who did so with excommunication! My wife, being one who liked to push the envelope a bit, tiptoed to the line of demarcation and stopped right at the border, leaning over it, trying to figure out what was so special about what lay beyond. Then one of her classmates pushed her from behind and she stumbled across into forbidden land. Shrieking, she dashed back, fleeing unknown terrors and certain eternal punishment. She survived, but the incident provided fodder for jokes and added to the mystery surrounding this place called Gethsemani.*

In my own exploration of Gethsemani, I've often wondered why I picked up The Seven Storey Mountain *in the first place. It may have*

Abbey of Gethsemani (1930s).

initially been just for show, like my earlier examination of Mao's Little Red Book. *That doesn't make too much sense, as the story of a Trappist monk wasn't exactly radical chic in the 1970s. I do know I was in a period of rootlessness and turmoil. Why I thought Merton had any answers I'm not sure. I do remember that it took me three or four attempts to get through the book. I'd check it out from the library, read a little, set it aside, get an overdue notice and return the book. A week or so later I'd return to try it again. I was getting the book from the main branch of the Louisville library, downtown at 4th and York streets. Later I would learn this was the library Merton used to frequent when he came to town for doctor's appointments or other errands. It's about two or three blocks from where he had his famous "4th and Walnut revelation."*

I was not experiencing much resembling revelation with the book. So much of what Merton described I could find no way of relating to, but as noted earlier the intensity and authenticity of his spiritual search touched me. After finally completing the book I decided to visit the place where Merton had lived his adult life.

As with Merton my first visit came at Easter weekend. Odd as it may sound it felt pretty adventurous to be going to a Trappist monastery for a weekend. This says something about my social life at the time, but also there just weren't as many people going to monasteries for retreats in those days. Driving the winding back roads south of Louisville, I wasn't sure what to expect. Finding the monastery presented the first challenge. I'd seen the film Deliverance *and my father had written for* The Beverly Hillbillies *and* Green Acres. *These rural, Southern stereotypes accompanied me as I wondered if I had made the right turn back where a sign simply read "Trappist." I rounded a curve, dipped into a small valley, and off in the distance there was a large church with an impressive steeple situated strategically on higher ground. It was a very dramatic departure from the modest homes, trailers, and barns I'd been passing. I'd seen great cathedrals in Europe and, while this didn't have the scale or grandeur of Notre Dame, I was impressed. Lancelot would* not be out of place here. Lawrence Cunningham would tell me later that Merton's first reaction to Gethsemani was that it "blew his mind." Looking back on my first visit, I understand the reaction.

I entered through a gatehouse that no longer exists. Rooms for retreatants were small, austere by American standards, not all that unlike rooms of youth hostels in which I had stayed in Europe. My strongest impression was that it was quiet, really *quiet*. It's amazing how much presence the absence of something can have. No phones, TV, radio, idle chitchat. Just silence.

I found my way to the church for a service I would later learn was Vespers. Silence was broken by the plainchant of the monks. It was the first time I had heard Gregorian chant. There were no booklets with which to follow along, so I had no idea what was being sung, but something about the singing hit home. Today I sometimes think about how these same psalms have been chanted for thousands of years by so many different peoples in such varied circumstances. On that first day these timeless stories of every human emotion touched something deep in me.

The next day, at the service of Holy Saturday, I watched in the dark from the balcony with other guests. It was all very new and seemed much like a play or a movie. Then to my surprise the wall of separation was broken. A monk came to the balcony inviting people to join the celebration in the main body of the church. I began to get up to follow him, but then at the last second changed my mind and sat back in my balcony seat. As the service went on I watched for a bit longer and then returned to my room.

I recently reread journal notes I made from that weekend. As I had prepared to return to Louisville on Sunday I had written, "It's time to leave. I take with me what I brought but I am not as I came." That stab at profundity is wince-worthy, but it does capture an element of the transformation that was beginning for me. Lawrence Cunningham says that Merton in his early conversion stages began to feel that "everything seemed connected." My memory of that first Gethsemani weekend was of remarkable moments where not only were things connected but, as I

47

later learned Julian of Norwich had said, all was well. I joined the
Roman Catholic Church six weeks later at Pentecost.

In making the documentary Soul Searching, *one of my primary*
goals was to make more accessible to a mainstream audience just what
Merton and his brother monks were trying to do at Gethsemani. I
know that his friend Bob Lax advised Merton to try to become a saint.
Merton himself was writing that he wanted to give everything to God,
to die to his false self. These sentences are written in plain English and
don't contain impenetrable theological terminology. Nevertheless, for
most they don't conjure meaningful images. To a reader in the postmod-
ern twenty-first century they can seem like pietisms. As my father might
have said, they seem like rationalizations for hiding away from the real
world. In my interviews I wanted the choir to bring life to what Merton
was attempting by embracing the monastic discipline.

Becoming a Monk

John Eudes Bamberger: Merton was full of enthusiasm when he came
to Gethsemani. But then after a time, and this happens to most people,
he had to confront the fact that he had brought a lot of baggage with
him that created problems. The monks at Gethsemani, on the whole,
lived a very simple life, and most of them were relatively simple people.
It was a completely different environment than Merton had been used
to. He had been associating with literary people and with artists from
the time he was five years old. On the very first pages of his autobiography he describes his parents as primarily artists, and because they were
artists they didn't altogether belong to this world. They were elevated
above the ordinary interests of this world. They had a vision, but it
didn't carry them far enough to bring them to God. So his parents lived
between heaven and earth as it were. In making that point at the very
beginning of the autobiography he is describing his own experience of

life. He had lived a very worldly life, and yet he wasn't satisfied with it, because he was aware there was something above the world that speaks to a person's soul. When he entered the monastery he had just found out that "Yes, it's God, and God is seeking me."

That's what monastic life is about. It's about transcending the world through training the interior senses that make you more perceptive of eternal reality. But it also delivers you, unlike art, which elevates you. You're dealing with a vision of reality that frees you from the senses in their mundane functions so that you can reconceive the deeper, hidden meaning of reality and give your life a new, fresh expression. Monastic life trains your senses to respond in such a way to this invisible world that you discover God and are delivered from the world. That's its purpose.

Many people think that there are certain types of personality that would be attracted to monastic life. I once had a candidate sent to me by a psychiatrist. The candidate was schizophrenic, and the psychiatrist thought that if you're a monk you've got to be somewhat schizophrenic. Actually, from my experience with live monks and with people who want to be monks, there's no particular type. There are some who are very introverted, and on the whole they would do less well than those who are more extroverted. Of course, those who are too extroverted would not be attracted to our life, but those extroverts who are attracted have to work at that because silence and solitude are an important dimension of monastic life. Maybe that's one reason why an extrovert would be attracted to monastic life: they're working to get a more balanced approach. Saint Benedict didn't write his Rule for Monks for people who have particular temperaments or particular characters but for those who were deeply committed to the search for union with God.

The American male conceives his identity as an independent person; he conceives his independence as taking initiatives, being his own boss as far as possible, and if it's not possible, he feels inhibited, his situation isn't as successful as it ought to be. So being independent is a major part of our sense of being an American man. It is taken for granted, and the more unconscious it is, the more influence it has on a man's sense of who he is or at least who he ought to be.

In the monastic life, it's not independence but freedom that a monk is seeking. It is a paradoxical freedom, however, because it is the freedom that comes from giving up your own will. Instead of seeking to affirm yourself, the monk seeks to bear witness to a truth that transcends him, transcends this world, and he seeks to become a servant of that truth, and that's what makes him free. Learning that, of course, is a lifetime job. I'm still working on it after fifty-five years as a monk.

Merton understood the kind of real freedom he was looking for very well early in his monastic life. In his autobiography he writes that becoming a Catholic and entering Gethsemani freed him from what he called "prisoners base." He understands that in order to attain to that kind of freedom he would have to die to this secular ideal of the successful man, the self-made man, the independent person. On the other hand there's a certain danger of passivity, of dependency, of falsity. There's no substitute for courage, for real inner freedom, for the energy that it takes to get liberated. All of those things are the monastic ideal, but they're threatened during the beginning period of becoming a monk when the new monk isn't too sure who he is.

Formation

Dom John Eudes's distinction between "independence" and "freedom" intrigued me. It challenges so much of what our Western culture sets up as valuable. More than once I've heard people say that monks are charming and admirable but they don't live in the "real" world. Who has the patent on reality, I wondered?

Soon after speaking with Dom John Eudes I was traveling in Southern California. I landed in the Orange County airport, which is named for John Wayne, an American icon if ever there was one. Outside the airport there's a larger-than-life statue of Wayne. He's dressed in cow-

boy regalia, posed in full swagger. Here's a man, for all I know a decent one, who never was really a cowboy or a Green Beret or ever saw combat that wasn't on a Hollywood backlot, yet he is revered as an American icon. Who has the patent on reality?

I was also struck by the manner in which Dom John Eudes talks of "courage" in the monastic life. It's a different type of courage than so many of our culture's icons evoke.

⥺ ⥺ ⥺

Dom John Eudes Bamberger: The first thing you have to do when you enter the monastery is do what you're told. If you don't want to do that, go someplace else. A novice has to believe that by living this life he is somehow going to be true to a vision that he has and that he brings with him when he requests to enter the monastery. Often this vision is relatively shallow and almost inevitably oversimplified. That's the first stage, though. You have to come and stay, and you can't do that without leaving your family, leaving your work, or leaving school, whatever you were doing, getting rid of whatever you had, at least temporarily.

Coming to a monastery begins with a willing choice the novice makes to be open because he's searching for something and has made what he feels are great sacrifices to get there. This stage teaches people to live in a situation where they don't have what used to make life sweet, even possible. You see, the early phase of monastic life is set up in such a way as to allow people to regress and to lose the identity they brought with them to the monastery. If you hold on to your old identity too strongly, you'll never become a monk. Or you might remain in the monastery, but you won't be formed as a monk. And it's threatening at first if you're not sure what's expected of you.

The same principle holds true if you go into the Marines. You're in a new situation, trained for a new mode of life, and you're under other people who seem to know what they are doing. That's why they are the ones picked to train you. Many leave the monastery in the novitiate

51

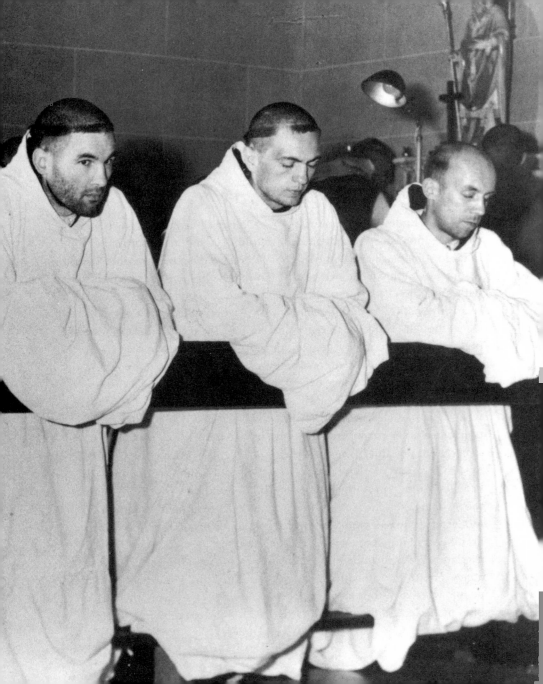

period because they're confused, but if they stick it out, they will be supported. The big work to be done for those in charge of novices is to help them use this confusion, and the passions they encounter, the feelings, the anxieties, the fears, the hopes, the attachments that they miss, and the temptations that they have, the resentment, the anger they may feel, to learn to make use of these experiences to understand that they're part of being who a person is. They're not an accident. You're full of passions you didn't know you had before you came. And you wouldn't have discovered them because you were successful where you were.

If they need too much affirmation and assurance that they're loved, I've advised men not to come with us. They won't get it. Living with men who have been bachelors all their lives, you're not going to get a lot of sympathy. You're not going to get a lot of attention. It doesn't mean they don't care about you; it's just the style. So helping people to discover who they are, how they're made, is the first step to helping them enter their hearts. It is paradoxical because it scares a novice. It often isn't pretty and very acceptable to the novice. A novice in a monastery soon discovers that, in Jung's term, he has a "shadow."

Being formed as a monk is being trained to live at deeper levels of your personality and to enter the deeper center of your heart. There are barriers that keep you from getting to the deeper center of your heart. There are things that we don't learn about life, because we've been able to get by through being clever, through being popular, and so on. So we never had to learn what it's like to work with somebody you can't stand, or who is very different, or who doesn't understand you.

In the world I got along well. I was popular, and so if somebody didn't like me, it was his problem, not mine. You know, that's our normal attitude. You don't think necessarily that way, but you respond that way to life. But in a monastery, if you don't get along with someone, and he's right next to you, and he's going to be there the rest of your

Thomas Merton (far right) at Gethsemani. It's quite a contrast with his three-piece suit, "big man on campus" days at Columbia.

life, you have to discover a way of happily dealing with someone like that. So you begin to learn about yourself, and it can seem like you've made a big mistake coming to the monastery. You've got more struggles there than you had when you were outside. When a novice thinks, "I'm in the wrong place," the novice master interprets that for him: "No, that's a sign you're making progress. You're discovering what you're really like. You're discovering what life can be like for people who don't have the possibilities you have had. You learn to identify with people who are forced to make life work, the poor and the limited. They have to spend their life in the village. They have to spend their whole life picking spinach, or whatever. I used to think of that when I was working in the garden. So that's the early stage of monastic life, and it's kind of critical. It's kind of like psychoanalysis in a way, but in a life setting.

The monastic life makes very heavy demands on an individual and his personal emotional life, so that it can't work in the long run properly unless you have an experience of God that means more to you than a family would mean, and a wife, children, your own home, your own business, your own profession, your own lifestyle, whether it includes playing golf or doing scientific research. All of those things are good. They have a strong appeal for some people, a very strong appeal that means everything to them until they experience something better. That's what I would say is the psychodynamics of monastic life. For it to work properly, you have to have had a personal experience of God that means more to you than anything else. And when that ceases to be the case, you may as well leave the monastery because you're not a monk anymore. You aren't living the life. The life consists in this very personal engagement of what's best in you with God, and what's important for God and other people. Unless you experience that, I think you'll either get sick, or fed up, or frustrated, or rebellious, and leave, or just feel it's not worthwhile.

All this remains true right up until at least the eightieth year of a monk's life. I'm in my eightieth year, so that's all I can speak of for sure. As Merton said once in class, "If it weren't for the resurrection of the

Lord," and he pointed out the window to the road, "I'd go out that road before Vespers today!" That's the way he said it, too. He meant it. It was in a course on St. Paul and his teaching on the resurrection. Merton said, "If it weren't for the resurrection of Jesus, I'd go up that road this evening."

Asceticism

Dom John Eudes explained the monastic life to me as no one ever had. He related how Merton explained the monastic life to novices with the same enthusiasm that some people have when talking about Notre Dame football. I believe Dom John Eudes has that same enthusiasm.

The penitential dimension so associated with Trappist life had initially mystified me. I've found I'm not alone in this. The austere life of a monk adds to their mystique just as self-denial separates them from our instant gratification culture. But does it serve a healthy purpose? I wanted to explore the Trappist emphasis on penance at the time of Merton's entry because people find it fascinating but also to make better sense of the practice and of Merton.

Anthony Padovano: I think that when Merton joined the Trappists there was in him a heavy sense of punishment that he felt that he needed to endure. I think some of it came from his realization that he had messed his life up badly, that the sex and the alcohol and the destructiveness on other levels had reached such proportions that they gave him a sense of self-disgust. I think that was intensified by the young woman that he had made pregnant and then abandoned. With good reason he should have felt a great deal of guilt over that and he did. When he turned to the monastery, to something pure and beautiful and simple and elegant, he felt he came there as a very spoiled, corrupted person, and that maybe incredible punishment would free him from that sense of guilt.

You get an insight into that in one of his early books on a Cistercian saint, Mother Mary Berchmans. She was a Trappistine nun who endured incredible kinds of deprivation and pain. She does things to practice penance that are clearly reckless, like keeping the windows open at night in Japan where she is and where it's bitterly cold in the winter, having clothes on that are all wet from doing the laundry, even though she is borderline tubercular, so she does not protect herself from the environment. Merton in his biography of her rejoices in all that. Merton thinks that's wonderful. Well, that's clearly neurotic and it's ill-advised. It's reckless but Merton can't see that then. He's writing this book the same year that he writes *The Seven Storey Mountain* by the way. Wonderful title he gave the book—*Exile Ends in Glory*. Everything after the title is downhill. It's not one of his better books by any means, but you do get an insight as to where he was at the time as regards penance. Doing penance was punishing. Of course that's coming out of the Christology and theology of that moment.

I think this idea, that there is a value in punishment and pain in their own right, is reinforced with a Christology that says that Jesus had to die and a theology that said that God wanted Jesus to die. The more painfully he died the better. I think that's dreadful. That's more Aztec theology, if you will, rather than profoundly Christian. But that's where Merton was and usually the people who choose a punishing God need that kind of God. That's not the God there is but the God that they require. I think that was true with Merton, but he did come to understand over the years that punishment doesn't serve any purpose. The point of all spiritual striving is love. Love will always bring with it wounds and pain and sacrifice and things of that nature, not because any of them are valuable in themselves but because, when love reaches certain boundaries, it can't get over them without feeling a sense of hurt or suffering. He did come to understand that better. In his mystical experience on the corner of 4th and Walnut streets, in the midst of humanity in Louisville,

Monks at worship at Abbey of Gethsemani.

56

his words are in the key of glory and not about sin and punishment. These kinds of experiences are at the heart of the discovery of God. The pain is only incidental.

Elena Malits: Merton went through a phase that is typical of new converts to Catholicism, and even more so of new converts to the monastic life. He felt he had to deny himself everything, including writing. Merton was told to write his story. Now I think he was delighted once he was told to do it, but he did not initiate that because he was going through this strict phase of everything. Thank God he was told to write his autobiography, because it not only provided him with an outlet but his story has meant so much to so many people. Merton was really a very expressive human being. In speech and in writing and in gestures he was not a restrained human being. If he had not had the opportunity to write, he would have had some kind of breakdown.

Lawrence Cunningham: Merton found a structure he needed in the monastic life. He found what he considered to be the most effective way to develop a deeper contemplative life. He found out, mainly through the good sense of his first abbot Dom Frederic Dunne, a way for his own writing to flourish. If you want to put it in religious terms, he felt that he was obeying the will of God for him in his life. He found the meaning of his life in leading the monastic life.

Jonathan Montaldo: Merton understood the efficacy of this serious life of prayer and work and silence. For whatever reasons, perhaps because he felt guilty, the austerity he endured at Gethsemani appealed to him, and life for the entire Gethsemani community was extremely austere. Merton obviously took to Gethsemani with great gusto. He loved the austerity and loved being a Trappist. He had found a home. He had found a community of real fellow travelers that he had never had.

Seven Storey Mountain

In talking with members of the Merton choir, I heard varied stories about how he came to write The Seven Storey Mountain. *Some said he was assigned the book as a task by Abbot Frederic Dunne. Others said Merton had been working up varied forms of the book for years. All agreed that the staggering success of the book surprised everyone.*

The book has become a classic, yet some people new to Merton have a difficult time relating to it, even more than I did thirty years ago. It is definitely of another time in American life and evokes the spirituality of another era. I thought that my documentary should place the book in context and try to capture what it meant to people at the time.

John Eudes Bamberger: Merton was convinced that he had something to say, and a way of saying it that the people of his generation would hear, that they would understand, that could speak to them. He had something to say that was meaningful. And he had that conviction very early at Gethsemani.

The ideal of the Trappist order was to live a hidden life, a retired life. In those days if you look at pictures that were taken of monks, they had their hoods up and their faces were averted. It was a life in which you were supposed to have disappeared from the world. And yet here's this twenty-eight-year-old monk writing his autobiography, as if he has a message for the whole world. Merton was convinced: "This is the way to preach the Gospel. This is the language that people can vibrate to." So he had to push that through, and at the end of his book he talks about disappearing into the monastery at the same time that he's writing his autobiography. It's not a contradiction but on the surface it looks like it. It is a paradox. He began to feel that writing was a gift God gave him and that it was his way of responding to a hidden vocation.

Paul Elie: Why was *The Seven Storey Mountain* a bestseller? It's hard to say. There are lots of factors. First is timing. It came right after the war when people were looking for answers. It came at a time when the Catholic public had, as some people tell it, emerged into the American mainstream, through the GI bill and through the assimilation of lots of immigrants from before the war. It was published by a major publisher. The timing was right in the sense that it was praised by Graham Greene and picked up by Evelyn Waugh, who had become a famous writer through his book *Brideshead Revisited*. But I think the real explanation for the autobiography's appeal is deeper than that.

The marketplace has its problems, but this was an instance of the bookselling public and the book-buying public recognizing that here was a truly original, strong, powerful book. There was nothing like it. There were tens of millions of American Catholics then with college degrees, but there was not a work of American Catholic literature of any great quality. Here comes this guy who is not even raised a Catholic who presumes to write a book that will explain Catholic America to itself in the terms of his own life. Well, Catholics looked at that book and said, "Here's a guy who thought so much of our tradition that he joined it." People outside Catholicism said, "Well, he's worth trusting because he wasn't raised with this religion that he converted to." All this is just a way of saying that the book had a rare authority and power. It wasn't like anything that had come before. It cleared a space for whole new ways of thinking about Americans and Catholicism.

Keep in mind that it's a book about a cloistered monastery. This is a book that took the reader to a place where he or she could not go. You couldn't pass beyond those walls unless you were a monk, except in rare instances. And here was a guy writing in a candid, matter of fact way, like a slight precursor to Holden Caulfield in J. D. Salinger's *Catcher in the Rye*, about what it was like to become a monk. Catholics and others alike were taken by the hand and shown this dark place by Thomas Merton in a way that they hadn't been shown it before.

There isn't any book today that is like *The Seven Storey Mountain*, but consider a book like *Angela's Ashes*. One year nobody's heard of Frank McCourt. The next year everybody has. Many, many people have read the book. Many who haven't read it intend to read it, or have heard about it or know the story. McCourt goes from being an ordinary person to a person with a public image in the course of a year or so. That's what happened to Thomas Merton. And that this should happen to a person who entered the monastery intending to die to the world and to not have any public image of any kind was exceedingly strange.

Lawrence Cunningham: After the Second World War America had a flourishing literature of religious writing by a number of people from a number of different perspectives. In the late 1940s Rabbi Joshua Liebman wrote a book called *Peace of Mind* that became a big bestseller in the United States. Catholic Bishop Fulton Sheen, who was the big radio and later a television guru, wrote a book called *Peace of Soul*. Both books are very American in a way: upbeat, affirmative, and therapeutic. Later, Norman Vincent Peale writes the mega-bestseller *The Power of Positive Thinking*. Now right in this period of the late '40s Merton writes *The Seven Storey Mountain*, and it's so totally unlike Liebman, Sheen, or Peale, because this is a book that is highly critical of secular life. Merton is turning his back on life in New York City. Even though he will later parody himself as having stomped on New York and tromped off to the monastery with the book of Revelation in his hand and John of the Cross in his hip pocket, his autobiography, in stressing asceticism, self-denial, and the sinfulness of culture, was a different variety of American bestseller.

Merton's book struck a big nerve in 1948. The war had been over for three years. We're going through a pretty good period in America. We're booming again, building up houses for the retuning GIs. Cars are being manufactured. It's being described by Henry Luce, owner of *Time Magazine*, as "the American Century." But people had had deeply bad experiences during the war and were not satisfied with American culture as it was. In the midst of America's postwar optimism, *The Seven Storey Mountain* was saying something powerfully important.

Robert Inchausti: What makes Merton such an important and interesting writer is that he's in the tradition of American writers who practice what they preach. So it's not so much that he has a clever use of words, or that he is a virtuoso with language. It's more that, because of his commitment to monasticism, he speaks out of an experience that is unique, and he is leading a kind of experimental life. The greatest American writers like Thoreau, Emerson, and Hemingway, and even later ones like Norman Mailer, have earned America's interest because they practice what they preach, and they write about their real experience.

Merton also had the additional gift of being able to articulate exactly what he was experiencing in terms of the ups and downs of his spiritual life and seeking. When you read Merton you have this odd experience of having been, sort of, found out, but set free at the same time. He sort of calls you on the very things that you yourself have experienced because he's experienced them, and then he sort of shows you how his contemplative monastic choices have given him a new perspective on that. That, I think, is what makes him so interesting and why people who read Merton usually are not attracted to one particular book. They begin with one book and then read everything he ever wrote. It is finally the voice, the person, the witness that you're attracted to, not so much the cleverness. He doesn't write fiction; it's all sort of autobiographical, spiritual self-revelation and introspection. Then, in his later years, when he brought those skills to bear upon his experiences and what we would call the real world, or the cultural world, he had a unique point of view, a perception that was just fascinating and compelled people's attention.

Merton struggled very hard his whole life to try to make that honest commitment to a life lived in accordance with conscience as far as he could see it. And then told us honestly the story of how that happened.

And then there is the credibility factor, being that he had gone to the Trappists and so all the money his books made was not for his own use. Merton had no purpose or reason to write other than to tell the truth about his own experience. There was no financial gain for him in any of this. This lends him a unique authority that you don't get with radio talk show people or television pundits who you know are getting paid to tell you the things that they are telling you, and whose own career and financial well-being depends upon them keeping the camera on themselves. So naturally they're going to tell you things that are self-affirming, self-aggrandizing, in line with their own ideologies. The effect that has on us as consumers is cynicism, a kind of wondering, where is reality in all this? We think we're sophisticated enough to resist these prejudices, but we're not. The media is stronger than our critical faculties. Things are misnamed. Things are called by the wrong names. So a writer's job is to say things as they are, call things by their right names. The magicians of language are the advertisers. The poets are the politicians. They're the ones who make illusions seem real. It's the writer's job to disarm the illusions and make reality real.

Merton, before he entered the monastery, wrote a few unsuccessful novels that made it clear that he was interested in spiritual self-understanding. He wrote poetry. But it wasn't until he got this assignment from the abbot to write the story of his life that he wrote *The Seven Storey Mountain*. He told a very personal story about how he transformed himself from an aspiring, modernist, avant-garde artist into a Trappist monk. He had transformed himself from being at war with his culture to finding freedom within it and love and support for and from the people around him. He had cured himself of his rebellious youth. In the 1950s he became master of scholastics and then master of novices at Gethsemani, which meant that he was in charge of the young novices who were entering the monastery, many who were coming back from World War II. In teaching them the monastic tradition, in teaching them the contemplative tradition, and teaching them to become monks, he realized that it wasn't just his story he had to tell. He had to tell the story of the monastery, he had to tell the story of Christ, he had to tell the story of this alternative approach to reality. His story became their story, and their story became our story.

And so that's when the transitions occurred: Merton realized it wasn't enough for him to tell the story of his own personal transformation, which of course is symbolic for everybody, but that he had to write essays and lectures that really explained it a little better. He understood that other people needed to be brought into the logic of it as well. You can see that in those books that he wrote in the 1950s that are more devotional classics, like *No Man Is an Island*, which for me signals the transition to "This is not just my story, this is our story." Then in the 1960s in *Conjectures of a Guilty Bystander*, he starts writing about nonviolence, about world politics, starts writing about the whole public scene and its relationship to the quest for authenticity that he himself had been struggling to achieve.

In talking with many monks of Gethsemani about living with Merton it was interesting to hear how thoroughly assimilated he was. Though the abbot made some concessions to Merton's writing, such as allowing a wider range of correspondence, there was little in the way of special treatment. I wonder if this lack of star status in the monastery didn't enable Merton to continue writing with his special affinity for "ordinary people." Though he laughingly referred to himself as "a duck in a chicken coop," he also worked at being part of the community.

Lawrence Cunningham: I do not think that Merton saw himself as a celebrity in the monastery after the success of his autobiography. The most obvious reason is that he had no sense of its success. He had no access to newspapers or magazines. He didn't know what *The New York Times* was saying about the book, if anything. He didn't have access to the media. Furthermore, the monks just saw him as another talented monk in the monastery. The royalty checks were going to the abbot, so it wasn't like all of a sudden a hundred thousand bucks was being dropped in his lap for having a bestseller. Communication with the larger world in monasteries of the 1950s was really limited.

John Eudes Bamberger: When I was reading his autobiography, I thought that he could not have written this book this well if he hadn't become a monk. Unless he had become a monk, he would not have found the same kind of fullness in his life to allow him to communicate so freely with so many different kinds of people in many different cultures. Merton was an artist. Everything in his autobiography has been not only thought through but transposed. He's not writing a historical chronicle. He's writing a life as experienced by someone who's spent a lot of time in contemplation, for whom the invisible world is the real world, and who is very keenly aware of communicating the values and the perspectives that he believes in, that are important for him. Merton told me, "You know, people get mad at me because the life here isn't the way they expected after they read *The Seven Storey Mountain*." That's not dishonesty; that's what art is about.

One day when I was in his office, he went over with me to view a reproduction of a landscape painting that he had on his wall. He said, "Now see, that's not what the landscape looked like. That's the way the artist painted it. He put this figure here for balance. It doesn't mean it was there." So that's the way Merton wrote, in my opinion. As I said before, in the opening pages of his autobiography he writes of art and the meaning of life. He saw life from an elevated perspective above its surfaces. So understanding his elevated view of the world explains what he had to go through when he was living with people who were doing farming and living as simply as possible. He had to make a very deep kind of renunciation of those elevated things that spoke to him. He experienced all the frustrations that accrue to that. So health problems developed that stayed with him throughout his life, physical problems probably caused in part by the stress that the kind of adaptation to monastic life he had to make put him under. That would be my judgment.

Obedience

For many the notion of monastic obedience is as unfathomable as that of penance. As one who came of age in the '60s I found it hard to imagine. My generational cohort gave great credence to virtually anything that questioned authority. Merton, with his ever-questioning, hungry mind, also squirmed under a tight rein. Yet time and again one hears or reads how seriously he took his vow of obedience as a monk. Dom John Eudes's drawing the distinction between "independence" and "freedom" in the monastic life helped me to understand better how Merton could find value in obedience. For me Merton's struggle with obedience, particularly as seen with his abbots, is one of the more interesting aspects of his life.

Father Maurice Flood is a former student of Merton's and presently the chaplain at Redwoods monastery in California. He laughs a lot. He laughs so much that at first I wasn't sure I could take him seriously. In explaining his take on monastic obedience he observed that most of us in the secular world lead lives of obedience without knowing it. He suggested our adherence to prescribed norms, schedules, or prejudices can be quite slavish and can create an unwritten "Rule" just as stern as Benedict's. Then he laughed. The joke is on us maybe.

Robert Inchausti: Many people wonder about Merton's vows of chastity, obedience, and poverty, and wonder why somebody with his talents, in particular his interests in writing, would subject himself to those kinds of obligations. Merton never saw them as obligations, but saw them as antidotes to his own worldly self, his own false self. So for him obedience, particularly, was a liberation from having to make choices based on his own careerist assumptions about where his life should go, or who he should be. Now in our modern mindset this could seem like an escape from responsibility, but Merton's having lived a wild youth let him see that, if he didn't have some ordering, he was capable of going in a million different directions. So it came to him as somewhat of a relief to subject himself to an external set of constraints and obligations that ordered his external life, so his internal life could explore its fullest reality. This makes sense only if you believe external reality is largely built on illusion and on worldly aspirations that may or may not turn out to be true. He was willing to take that leap and say, "OK, I'm going to give up on the externals for the sake of the internals and find reality that way." On the whole, obedience was a great grace for Merton. Left on his own, he probably would have lived a very bohemian existence through which he would always be testing the limits. Obedience was his way of turning it around and saying, "OK, here are the limits." Most of his obedience involved daily life kinds of constraints that we all deal with.

Anthony Padovano: There were three abbots during Merton's time. There was Frederic Dunne, the abbot of the monastery at the time when Merton was received. There was James Fox for twenty of the twenty-seven years. Then there was Flavian Burns, who had been a novice under Merton. So there were three abbots. One was a surrogate father, Frederic Dunne, who understood Merton. [Dunne] told [Merton] to do something that had never been done before in a Cistercian monastery, to write an autobiography of his own life. It was incredibly daring for Frederic Dunne to do something like that because Cistercians were supposed to write very safe books that one could care less about.

Dunne dies very unexpectedly and the next abbot was light years different from Merton in character and temperament. [Fox's] way of thinking was still very much in a business frame of mind, which is very different from Merton who is the son of painters and is a poet. So you have diametrically opposed temperaments for one thing.

James Fox told me, "When I became abbot the financial situation at Gethsemani was awful. They were ready to sink financially." That's when he brought in all the cheese and fruitcakes and jellies and assembly lines. That was antithetical to Merton. He thought that's the last thing a Cistercian monastery should be doing.

Both of them were right, but they didn't fully see that, I think. You can't satisfy a mortgage payment with a lyrical poem. Bankers are not moved by that. On the other hand, without the poetry and commitment to the contemplative life something vital about Cistercian existence would be lost. They were fated to be at odds with each other.

I think also that Fox's spirituality was very conservative, and he just could not understand what Merton was all about. He said to me, "I tried to stop the writing." And I said, "Why would you have done that?" And he said, "I understood Merton the monk. I didn't understand Merton the writer." And I said, "But the two of them belong together. If the writing stopped he would've stopped being a monk. They were really connected." He said, "I never saw that and I never endorsed that."

So he's trying to stop Merton from writing, which is the very thing that is Merton's oxygen. That would cause other problems. And I said, "Well why did you value, how did you value, Merton the monk?" And he said, "Well I felt I had to keep him within the lines of Cistercian rule and spirituality." He said, "You know, he was the one I went to for confession." I said, "I find that astonishing. Why would you have done that with someone whom you disagreed so thoroughly?" He said, "Because I knew he was the best."

So it was a very complicated dance, so to speak, that was going on.

James Conner: John Cassian, who was one of the very early monastic writers in the fourth century, says in his writings that the whole purpose and goal of the monastic way of life is to bring a person to what he calls

Abbot James Fox.

purity of heart. And in that he does not mean purity in the sense of chastity, he means purity of heart in the sense of a heart really open to God, open to other people and free of the encumbrances that we all have. It's always been said that basically even the original sin, in the Garden of Eden, with Adam and Eve, was this desire on their part to want to, as Genesis says, "be like God." They wanted to develop what was a false self, on their part, and not to recognize the fact of their complete and utter dependence on God. And so real purity of heart, then, is when we can come to that point of realizing that we are creatures of God, we are children of God, and that we are called upon to allow God to be the dominating and motivating force within our own lives. And everything, then, which will militate against that, is something that we have to try to root out in one way or another. So Benedict makes the main cornerstones for that work his chapters on silence, on obedience, and enclosure. And all three of those may seem to be a rather negative thing, but they're geared to bring us to that point of real purity of heart. A freeness from that drive toward a false self.

Certainly it is much more difficult for a person of the twentieth century to undergo this transformation because the whole of society, the whole thrust of human growth and human development and human potential is geared almost in the opposite way. Especially in our modern society in the Western world, it becomes almost simply a dog-eat-dog mentality. And again, that's the exact opposite of what St. Benedict would speak of or what John Cassian would speak of, or even what the gospels would speak of.

Lawrence Cunningham : Abbot James Fox had a certain vision of obedience and of the monastic life. He combined in his persona a kind of a sentimental piety with a tough-minded way of managing the monastery. He wanted Gethsemani to have a high profile. He wanted it, as he described it one time, to be the West Point of monasteries, the best of the very best. He valued Merton as a member of the monastery and trusted him with very important offices, such as master of novices, one of the most important jobs you can get in the monastery. At the same time he did not want Merton to become a public persona outside the monastery. He didn't want him traveling, didn't want him being interviewed, and he didn't want him going off and giving talks. He was kind of tough on him that way.

Merton was a mercurial kind of person, in the sense that he could get an idea one day, it's the greatest idea that he's had in ten years, and then two days later he would be talking about something else. Then sometimes he would want to put his ideas into play. For example, we know in the late 1950s he had this idea of going to Latin America and having a hermitage, or a small simple monastery. I know this period very well because I edited his journals of that period. That was a crazy idea. This was a guy who couldn't drive a car, he couldn't keep his contracts straight, and he was hopeless at organization. He was always months late in getting mail. He needed to be in the structured life. The idea that Thomas Merton was going to go off and found an experimental monastery was just unthinkable. It was just an idea that he had. Everyone has these fantasies, "Oh, I would really like to go off and spend the rest of my life living on the beach."

John Eudes Bamberger: Dom James Fox had a very simple idea of the monastic life, and he was capable of living that, but few other people were. Dom James had terrific willpower. He was a very sophisticated person, but he was also complex. I think that's why he was, in a way, more paradoxical than Merton. Dom James's friends, people he had been students with, were the vice president of Pan American and the head of General Motors in France. So that was one side of the abbot, knowing Wall Street inside and out and yet living this life of poverty and simplicity and very few ideas. So when it came to writing, and the intellectual life in general, Dom James felt, "Well, if you're a real monk, you don't need all that. All you need is to love God and carry the cross." That's what the monk in him really felt, but he was also intelligent. He encouraged me to go out and study psychiatry. And he supported

Merton in his writings. That doesn't mean he appreciated it. It was sort of, "Well, if this is what you feel you're supposed to do, go ahead and do it." But he told me once, "There was only one thing and one time that I asked Merton to write, and I think it was for a meeting someplace. For the rest, he was free to write or not."

Dom James was not a very articulate, analytical kind of person, but he was shrewd and he was intuitive. He could look and see things and their implications in a finger snap when other people were just all confused without being able to recognize opportunities or problems. Well, Dom James had a lot of that to him. He also was very intelligent but not analytically inclined so that it could seem that he was rather simple. He was motivated by actually a few simple ideas that were oversimplified for most of us, but he lived them. Merton said that. I remember hearing him say once, "Dom James has too few ideas, but he lives them."

I wouldn't say that Dom James understood all of the ins and outs and nuances of Merton. He didn't, and he thought it would be a waste of time to get involved with all of that. I think he really felt that a lot of what Merton did was sort of a waste of time or an evasion or something. But he understood the conditions for Merton's following what were essentially his best interests, and he understood those conditions better than Merton did in certain areas. For example, he once told me in private, when we were discussing some invitation from a cardinal for Merton to come to a meeting, "If Father Louis starts that, he'll get too involved, and he'll lose his mystique, and lose the influence that he can have for good with people, because he'll become like every other smart person who's talented. Now he has a special message." This is the way he saw it. Even though he was under pressure from Rome, a cardinal writing and saying Merton should do this, Dom James wrote back and said, "I don't think that's in line with our vocation." Period. And he knew Merton wouldn't like it or understand it, but then he would say, "You know, that's not the real Merton. He'll come around."

Merton never really had a father, you know, who was fatherly. I think Dom James understood that side of his needs. Merton needed somebody to direct him. It could easily look like manipulation, but I think there was much more to it than that, and I think Merton understood that.

Jonathan Montaldo: James Fox and Merton might often have experienced tension with one another, but James Fox in 1955 appointed Merton Gethsemani's novice master. That's one of the most important jobs in the monastery. Here is the person who's going to instruct all of the new people to blend in with the Abbey of Gethsemani's culture, and he picks Merton and supports his having the position for ten years from 1955 to 1965. There are those who say that Merton needed James Fox. He needed someone to keep the reins on him. Someone who sympathized with him, saw his talent, saw his genius, saw his profitability for the monastery, of course, but also realized that this was a man who needed reining in. Merton would come in enthusiastic about a plan and James Fox reportedly would say, "Let's give it a month of thought," because he knew in a month Merton would have a new plan. Merton even wrote in his journals toward the end of his life that he needed Dom James and that Dom James was good for him.

Merton was Dom James's confessor for a time. The abbot of Gethsemani went to confession to Thomas Merton. Now that's a tribute to both of them. It was Monica Furlong in her biography of Merton who wrote—and she is alone in assuming this, I think—that Fox ruined Merton's intellectual and spiritual career, that he kept Merton hemmed in so as not to lose a profitable asset for the monastery. I think she misread their relationship completely. I never met James Fox, but my understanding is that, after the Furlong biography, he never tried to set the record straight. When James Fox wrote about Merton publicly, he only wrote approvingly. He never tried to say, "Look, I'm getting a bad rap here." Much to his credit.

Christine Bochen: What I know of James Fox I know through Merton's eyes. And a little bit more as people who knew James Fox reflect on him. It seemed to me that the most remarkable thing that I ever heard was a story that William Shannon shared with me in a conversation that he had with Dom James Fox, who described Merton as the most obedient monk he had known. Now that might not be verbatim, but certainly the thought is there. So I think about James Fox as, in one way, Merton's nemesis, and in another as a kind of guide in the spiritual life in the sense that the abbot came to define for Merton a framework in which to be a monk. He created, much to Merton's dismay sometimes, the kind of framework in which Merton was able actually to move and do what he wanted to do. If we read the journals, we find Merton sometimes very petulant and sometimes whining about Dom James, yet Dom James provided for Merton the kind of—security isn't the right word—but provided for him a kind of stability, but I don't want to use that word either in this context. He made it possible for Merton to be creative. "Structure" is the word that I want.

Dom James provided for Merton a structure and in many ways protected Merton and allowed him to be who he needed to be. He understood Merton better, perhaps, than Merton thought he did, and Merton's attempts to go "off the rails," as one of his school friends from his early years in Oakham School in England said, were contained by Dom James, and in the process gave Merton a structure in which he could work creatively.

Paul Quenon: Merton had a deep loyalty to the life and deep commitment to the vows as we take them and was faithful. He lived in the dialectic between the need to grow and develop and the need to live the life as it is. He was always expanding. He was always pushing the boundaries and yet he knew he had made a vow of obedience, subjected himself to the discernment of the abbot, and he was true to that. He would try to push it sometimes, but when push came to shove he would yield. I remember Dom James once saying about Fr. Louis, I don't know how it came up in the conversation but he said, "Basically, he was humble." And I think that's quite a tribute because you know Dom James had to put up with an awful lot. And Merton had to put up with a lot from Dom James too for that matter. They were very different types. They just had a different concept of what church life is, what it should be. You kind of think sometimes, "Merton deserved a better abbot than what he got," but maybe he got just the abbot he deserved. You would think he should have had somebody who had more imagination, who had more creativity, who could experiment in new forms of monastic life. There are people like that in France and I don't know if there were any like that in this country at the time. There might have been. You would hope that there could have been an interaction there but it never happened. As a result we have in Merton the witness of somebody who struggled with the limitations of church life and religious life and yet still made it a very creative thing and a very powerful thing.

James Conner: If we are really willing to die to ourselves or to be transformed, the best way that monastic tradition says this is achieved is through obedience. And it's obedience not just in a sense of having to do what somebody else tells you to do; ultimately it's an obedience which brings us to a radical surrender of self to God. And we surrender to God through the visible person—the abbot, the novice master, the spiritual father—with whom we are working. And so that's why obedience became very important. And it was important in Merton's way of forming the novices, but it was equally important for himself.

And at the same time it was not something that came naturally to him. Merton struggled a great deal with it, perhaps more than many if not most of the monks at that time did. The very fact that he had strong feelings and strong ideas and strong convictions about certain things meant that rather frequently he would clash either with the abbot, with other members of the community, or the Order. Not in a way that he would lose his temper, or that he would do or say anything blatantly improper, but in a way that you could tell he was having a real struggle within himself. Of course perhaps one of the major areas that has been written about in that whole aspect of his own inner struggle with obedience was his dealing with the abbot at that time, Dom James Fox. Both men were very strong personalities. Both men had very definite convictions and ideas. Dom James's whole spirituality was very much centered around the aspect of the crucifixion. His motto as abbot was *Deo crucifixus*, which was "God crucified." And he expected in a real way that all of us would come to that point of following Christ in that willingness to be crucified, particularly through obedience.

Merton, on the other hand, was not so tied to one particular mystery of Christ. For Merton, I think, there was more simply the person of Christ himself and the reality of the life that we are called to live in God. And consequently he was able to take much more of a consideration and appreciation of the way that our own human element enters in, so that it's not simply a question of constantly squelching that human element but of finding how to direct it, how to gear it in a certain way. One of the major areas that the two of them differed in was the whole issue of enclosure. Merton would have liked very much to be able to travel much more than he did. But Dom James Fox was particularly adamant that Merton was to remain within the monastery. Some of that was based on Dom James's own fear of human nature, in particular Merton's human nature, because if you've read *The Seven Storey Mountain*, you realize that his earlier youth was somewhat wild. It was not that monastic, to say the least. And I think that Dom James had that fear that if he'd turned him loose, in going outside, that he would revert to something like that.

To that extent, it was really an issue that he basically didn't trust Merton enough to be who he strove to be within the monastery. And I think that in itself hurt Merton even more than just the question of the stringency of obedience, the fact that he felt Dom James really didn't fully trust him on one level. On most other levels Dom James trusted Merton completely. He trusted him enough that he entrusted himself to him by choosing Merton as his own confessor for the sacrament of reconciliation regularly. And Merton regularly would go see Dom James even apart from the question of confession. The two kept in very close contact. While there were very definite differences, both showed a tremendous respect for one another.

Father John Dear brought an interesting perspective to Merton. He is a Jesuit priest much in the mold of his friend and mentor Daniel Berrigan. Because of his fervent commitment to social justice, he often finds himself at odds with authority. His recounting of how Merton's struggle with obedience has helped him was very moving and instructive.

John Dear: The whole question of obedience is very mysterious. It's almost like a medieval practice, you know, going back to the Middle Ages with the Benedictines and then of course later to the Trappists and the Jesuits and all the religious orders. As part of religious life you're professing vows of poverty, chastity, and obedience in community. The theory and the theology is that we're a community of servants of God and we're almost a nonviolent version of the military, that we're all going to be a team together and work on one thing. With the Trappists it's going deep into the life of prayer. With the Jesuits it's into the world working for peace and justice, but always as a team and following the team leader and praying that God is really, really using us.

Obedience is very hard and very painful. Here's Merton who's such a brilliant intellectual, worlds ahead of anybody else, going through the humility of obedience under an abbot in community. This is a very powerful and mysterious witness. And then he starts speaking out like a true prophet, denouncing war, segregation, nuclear weapons, what the country is doing in Vietnam. Nobody could understand this and so finally they just invoked holy obedience and said, "Merton, you're not allowed to write anymore about that." So Merton knew that his life was rooted in God and that he was part of a global community of Christians, monks, people of prayer. He didn't want to bring scandal to them. He wanted to be part of the worldwide community and to play his role and, if what he was doing was truly the will of the God of peace, then he could write this and he knew that, "Well, if it's not published in my lifetime, if God wants these teachings on peace and justice to come out, they eventually will and bear good fruit." Here we are, all these decades later, still talking about Merton, and more people are reading Merton than throughout his lifetime, so he was right.

Now it's hard! It goes against everything in our American culture, you know, that you would obey somebody who doesn't understand what you're doing, but the wisdom is, ultimately that we're obeying God. If we can just be humble, modest, and faithful, stay with the truth and speak gently as best we can, whether writing or speaking out, or some people getting, you know, involved in public demonstrations, however we're called, but be part of that global community, it will bear good fruit.

Merton has helped me stay a Jesuit and in the church. Every time I get in trouble for speaking out publicly as a churchperson against war and nuclear weapons and other injustices, every time I get called in or yelled at, which happens a lot, I think about Merton. He just stayed put and was faithful and he didn't make a scene. He kept trying to go to the roots about what it means to be a monk and a priest and a Christian and trusting that, if this work is really the work of God, then God will take care of it in God's good time. That's a hard lesson to learn and I'm still trying to learn it. I may not be able personally to actually make a big difference or end war and nuclear weapons, but if this is the work of God, then it will end up bearing good fruit and one day nuclear weapons will end up being abolished and wars will end. So Merton gives me courage to stay the course, and I need all the courage I can get.

We will never know what Thomas Merton went through, the heat that he suffered for writing these great books and meeting with so many people about war and racism and then nuclear weapons. Especially his stance on the Vietnam war, because he was so far ahead of his time. He must have suffered personally, and he certainly suffered from his Order who were trying to suppress him and telling him to be quiet. He began suffering criticism from around the country, from New York's Cardinal Spellman, the vicar general of the U.S. Military who traveled to Vietnam to bless the troops, and from Catholic newspapers around the country who were denouncing Merton. He got all these letters saying, "What happened to this nice pious monk who wrote these beautiful books about the seeds of contemplation? Hey, why are you talking about nuclear war? What does that have to do with religion?"

Teaching

Earlier I mentioned my curiosity about the crucified Jesus I first saw in a Catholic church as a child. The positive aspects of suffering eluded me and are still something with which I struggle. In Soul Searching *I didn't want to depict Merton as someone who simply trudged through his monastic life, enduring hardship but finding little or no consolation. Reading his journals it's evident there were great joys in his monastic life. He would grumble about many things but also wrote often of the happiness in his life at Gethsemani. The great smiles captured by photographers like Ralph Meatyard, John Howard Griffin, and Ed Rice show a man capable of tremendous joy. I wanted* Soul Searching *to show "consolations" aplenty. One was his role as a teacher, both of his students at the monastery and also of his readers.*

ᔥ ᔥ ᔥ

John Eudes Bamberger: The first impression I had of Merton as a teacher was when I was a novice. Just a few months after I had entered the monastery, I heard he was giving a series of lectures and that the novices were expected to attend them. It was his enthusiasm for the spiritual life that marked his teaching. He spoke of the spiritual life the way a lot of people that I had been acquainted with spoke about Notre Dame football. I went to Notre Dame, and Merton had the same kind of enthusiasm about the life of prayer, about meeting God, about monastic life. "This is it, men, you're lucky to be in a place where you can devote yourself to what really counts. This is the way to live." He would talk about God and prayer that way, like we were at a football rally. He had that kind of enthusiasm and spontaneity, no airs at all, very simple and natural. When I read his books, prior to becoming a monk, I thought he might be, not a snob exactly, but that he moved in high intellectual circles, knew Mark Van Doren, one of the best literature teachers in the country, but there was none of that in Merton's teaching style day by day. That speaks to young people. All of the young monks liked Merton. He gave you an image of what a monk should be like. You should learn to love God from your heart, naturally. Piety isn't something you put on when you go to church, it's a way of life, and prayer flows out of life and has life as its content.

So that was the beginning of being a student of his, and he maintained the same natural style of teaching all the years I knew him. When I was a junior monk, after the novitiate and my first vows, he became our teacher—master of scholastics. He took his preparation for class very seriously. He always had many more notes than he could deliver. In fact many of his class notes would turn into articles later on. He'd write them up. It was clear he had thought through his ideas about prayer, about God, about life, about relations with other people, with society. His ideas in class weren't just spontaneous reactions: they were based on serious, analytical thought and they fit into an overarching view of life and its meaning. Both of those dimensions were there. He had a method of study that was relatively scientific. I had, of course, had training before I came to the monastery, and I could see his method. He got me interested in studying the Fathers of the early church and the Bible. He also had interests in French literature and was reading French magazines. He made me realize that there's a lot you can't get at unless you know French. So in these ways and others, Merton formed me and helped me integrate various aspects of monastic life.

His chief influence as a teacher came from his personal involvement and enthusiasm. The fact that he always spoke with great personal investment, with a lot of spontaneity, and with emotional involvement made his classes interesting and highly personal. He was clear, organized, always well prepared, very enthusiastic, and was interested in the students. So I got a great deal out of his teaching, and I think my attitude was typical of the whole class. We had about twenty-eight to thirty-two scholastics, all three years of the juniorate, the monks in first simple vows. I don't remember any of the students who complained about him as a teacher; I think all of us liked him. In fact he was very popular. You wouldn't get this impression from some of his more acerbic comments about the community in his journals, but he was very much appreciated and liked, especially by the younger people.

Maurice Flood: He was very down to earth, but enthusiastic. Sometimes he would wonder if we were getting anything out of what he was saying. He would say, "Well, I don't know about you guys, but I'm getting a lot out of this because I've had to do research and get ready for these talks." That's a marvelous thing for a teacher to say, that he is getting a lot out of pouring himself out and teaching us about ancient monasticism, our Order, and what we're faced with in modern times.

He taught us how to retain our humanity, our humanness. When I entered the Trappists that was the one thing it seemed you were supposed to diminish. You were supposed to put down as much as possible your humanness, and be almost like angels. I think he said we were created as human beings; God already created the angels, so don't try to be angels, just be human, a human person seeking the divine. And this is going to take a long time, years, so don't take yourselves too seriously or else you're just going to burn out. That may not have been his exact words, but he said, you know, go easy on yourselves, be serious but don't take yourself, your own ideas or your own impor-tance, too seriously. It will take care of itself. I remember him saying, "You come to the monastery and, after a few months, or a half a year or so, you think, 'Oh, this is difficult,' and then after a year or so more, you think, 'Oh, this is *very* difficult,' and after another year or so, you think, 'This is impossible!'" So that's the way it should be. You just find that, if you have to do it yourself, the monastic life is impossible. You have to surrender to the monastic discipline and just trust that it will work out.

I remember him as very humble and direct. He did not look down on us; he just taught us as fellow monks, so that helped to open us up, make us not look at him but on the vision he was telling us about, of God, of the divine, and the wonder of nature. I remember once he took a bunch of us for a walk in the woods one Sunday and we stopped and sat down and he discovered that one monk had brought a book, and he said, "Why did you ever bring that book with you, because 'the book' is all around you. You have your books back in the monastery but you shouldn't have to bring one here." Probably the monk just thought maybe it would get kind of boring out there, and he would have time to read, but that was a good point about how your books are necessary but not at this point in the woods with each other.

Paul Quenon: I think the novice master is one of the most important jobs in the monastery, because he's in charge of the formation of the new people who come in. So it really requires everything. You have to deal with educating the person. You have to give spiritual direction. You have to be an example of the monastic life yourself. You have to deal with the abbot and officers in the community, all of whom have ex-pectations of you as novice master. But Fr. Louis said it was the best job in the monastery, and he really enjoyed it, I think.

He had to give conferences two times during the week and then on Sunday in the afternoon. The midweek conferences were usually half an hour. Rather short. You know, he'd sit down and get to the point and then it was over. On Sunday we had more time, so he could sort of spread out, and that's when he did his Scripture commentaries. His other big responsibility was to give spiritual direction to the novices, and that involved a visit maybe every other week. Spiritual direction might be anywhere from half an hour long, but could run overtime to an hour. It usually did with me because we liked to talk.

He was a natural teacher. His material was well prepared, but he was spontaneous. And he never got through his notes. There was always more on his notes than he had time to deliver, but he wasn't rushing things. He would go through cycles of presentations and have to repeat himself. Like he would do St. Bernard and then after two years a new group was coming in and he would start St. Bernard again. So if you happened to be in the novitiate during an overlapping period you had that material from before, but it still always seemed new. I mean he had rethought the thing and added material or had different insights on it. So it was always pretty interesting. I didn't find him boring and he was always spontaneous. Anybody who's heard his tapes is always surprised at how much laughing there is going on. And he had imagination. So I wouldn't say it was dry at all.

Whatever subject he talked about, he usually came around to its concrete application to the monastic life. It's obvious how it applies to us when he spoke about the Cistercian Fathers. But he could also be talking about the Sufi mystics and how this applies to us. How what they do is what we ought to be doing. In fact we are doing it but we just don't appreciate it in that regard. Like the theme of "dying to self," for instance. He would find that theme outside of Christian traditions and he would say, "This is what we're about, too."

One thing I'd like to mention, though, is that on Sunday afternoons often he would give commentaries on Scripture. He was shy of critical exegesis. It was still a new thing in the monastery, but what he was doing is actually now considered the most up-to-date approach. He would take the book of Scripture just as a piece of literature and analyze it from that. Just take it as a text that's in front of you without trying to determine historical value and things like that. How does this text help us understand the way of God in our lives? And he was able to do it with a literary flair. His commentary, for instance, on the book of Job was memorable.

The most important thing he taught me was how to love God and how to be true and honest in the presence of God. Not to fake it, just to be yourself and live in such a way that you know God accepts you and you go from there. Mostly he taught by example. There was no method. He never taught a method of prayer. Some people are surprised when they come to Gethsemani and ask, "Aren't you given instruction in meditation?" No, we aren't, because we live in a sort of a Montessori school. You have a conditioned environment and then out of that grows spontaneous reflection, meditation, gratitude, prayer. He never gave any instructions except, "Quiet down. Spend time in front of the Blessed Sacrament." Or "Go to the woods and just be quiet. Take a book and reflect on it." Things like that. Real simple. It'll happen. That's the way he did it. And we just sort of went with that.

As the novice master, I think he certainly had a sense of discipline. It was popular to criticize the trivial rules of the monastery, and he never made a big deal out of that. He said, "Well, just keep the rules and forget it. Don't make a big issue out of it." And he expected you to keep silence. I remember one time I was sitting in the scriptorium and there was another novice there and he was my age. We were both young. We were supposed to be reading our books, but we got to making signs and then of course whispering with our signs. Well, he walked in and he said, "Well, you guys are supposed to be keeping quiet." Then he left. Well, he came back again after about twenty minutes and there we were, you know, whispering and making signs. He said, "You're going to have to keep silence better than that if you want to stay in the monastery." So he had definite expectations.

Merton teaching novices.

Merton would have been a critic in any situation. If he had stayed in the world, he would've been somebody who had an eye for the flaw. But being in the monastery he was operating out of an experience, a tradition, and had much more of a basis than just your average intellectual might have. So he was forever apologizing for talking like somebody who has authority. But somebody who is blind about their authoritarian voice is suspect. He was not blind about having a voice of authority. He was trying to balance and correct it and condition it and didn't always succeed, maybe, but he had a kind of assurance.

A person who has real authority speaks from the heart; they speak out of the center, the core of their being. Well you have to be in touch with the core of your being to begin with. That's what the monastic life gives you. It brings you back to yourself, your true self. You become your true self and, when you can speak from the true self, you're going to have authority whether you know it or not. That came through with Merton.

Dom James made the most of emphasizing that we are at the pinnacle, that we have been given this extraordinary gift of living a Trappist / Cistercian life, a life of prayer, silence, solitude, and seclusion. We really felt that we were on top of the heap after one of his conferences. There was a certain amount of complacency in that, an unwillingness to look critically at the limitations of our life or the ways that people might just thoughtlessly be going through a routine. Dom James could make you feel very content, and he was trying to get you to feel content because he wanted you to stay in the monastery. But Fr. Louis was willing to knock the life and knock this thing or that thing. He wanted you to live this life by choice, consciously, and not to accept mindlessly everything that goes on.

James Conner: As a teacher he was very, very well prepared certainly, in the talks and the conferences he would give. At the same time he had a real gift of being able to ad lib, to be able to talk off the top of his head, and to inject a fair amount of humor. A number of people remarked, in listening to the tapes that have been published, that you get a whole different view of Merton in listening to the tapes than you do in reading the books. Because there's more an element of that spontaneity, more an element of that humanity, of that sense of humor, that comes out. I think the main thing with Merton as a teacher, which he was very, almost adamant about, was the fact of people not trying to play one-upmanship with him in his conferences and the like. He could be almost curt and short with someone if he sensed that that's what they were trying to do.

Merton's "students" extended far beyond the walls of Gethsemani. Over the years I've met countless people from every walk of life who have been shaped by Merton's writing and life example. With almost all of his books still in print his instruction continues.

Kathleen Deignan: I suppose that I have been a student of Thomas Merton's since the nuns in high school put the first book of Merton's in my hands. I have to say that he inspired me to journey somehow along his route. At this stage of my life with him I'm discovering what one might call the creation mystic in Merton. He is a teacher in such a broad way that I'm not sure that I could just say that he is my master as a master of creation spirituality. I think I love Merton's profound understanding of the human soul in God, the human soul hungering, yearning, questing for God, for the divine life that in our tradition we say is the promise, which we have seen embodied in Jesus. Merton's love of Christ and his way of recovering and retrieving a tradition is often not presented to us in ordinary engagements with our churches. At least that's not my experience. One needs to go searching more deeply for the spiritual masters who will help us awaken the life of the soul so that we can be about this transformation to Christ. Merton makes this process so accessible, so vivid, so actual and real. I say this as a professor of theology.

I've just had the joy of teaching sixty-four young college students a course on the writings of Thomas Merton. I could have cried oftentimes; I could have wept before my students, hearing them talk about the awakening of their contemplative lives, inspired and provoked by reading Merton. To hear students, as I heard yesterday, talking about wanting to practice silence more deeply, because in the practice of silence one could hear the difference between the voice of the false self and the voice of the true self, that true self that's always summoning us into the depths of intimacy with God.

To hear young college students who had never ventured to talk this way, particularly in front of each other, begin to talk about their contemplative lives, to talk about their lives in God, is a wonderful thing. I think I am most appreciative to Merton for that in my own life. Then for all of the other avenues that he beckoned me to explore, to really take my life in the world seriously and to be faithful to this paradise that he says is all around us, all we need do is enter in. So I think for me Thomas Merton is the great teacher of the mystical life and he just knows where it is, he sees it in all its dimensionality, and he can bring us there through the vitality of his literary gift.

Robert Inchausti: Ralph Waldo Emerson said that he had one truth that he was going to teach and that was the infinite value of the individual soul. That was Emerson's truth. He said, "Whenever I can convince someone of the infinite value of their own personal soul I have succeeded in all my arguments." Merton is similar to Emerson in that he believes in the infinite value of the individual soul, but in one of his books he said, "But I also have another message, which is that the nothingness that we fear, that we try to defend ourselves against, through accomplishments, through diversions, through entertainments, through worry, is nothing to fear." That nothingness is really the worldly face of the being of God. And that one can move into nothingness, one can give up everything, one can lose everything, and there's still reality, and there's still God. That should be reassuring to someone in the midst of a world that is threatening to take everything away from them. The truth is that the world can't take away what is most essential in you. It can't take away "being." Failure can't take away "being." Failure can't take away God. That is a reassuring message from somebody who gave it all up, so he's not just talking through his hat. He's not just saying it's easy for me because I don't have a mortgage. He's saying, "Yeah, I don't have a mortgage, I don't have anything, and I'm fine."

Henry David Thoreau is sort of the same way. When Thoreau went to Walden, he came back a couple of years later and lived in town. One of the questions they asked him was, "Well, if it was so great living out in the country, why don't you stay in the country, why did you come back into town?" He said "Well, I learned my lesson from Walden that I don't need anything in the town. Town doesn't bother me anymore. If I lost my job, if they rode me out of town, I could go back to Walden and live very happily. I'm free." That's what Merton ultimately gives us, a kind of intellectual, spiritual freedom that most other writers aren't generous enough to give us. They haven't given up their art or their fame. They're holding on to something which makes us wonder as souls, "What would happen to me if I didn't have that?" So I think that's Merton's monastic contemplative good news, if he has any.

And then, once that's arrived at, now let's look at the culture. Let's look at Tidy Bowl commercials. Let's look at the monks I live with. Nothing is above critical observation, not because I'm a nihilist but because I'm not a nihilist, because I know that there's something real underpinning everything, that's independent of all these things. So I think that's why he can dialogue with anybody, he can dialogue with atheists and he can dialogue with Eric Fromm and the Dalai Lama and Thich Nhat Hahn and Paul Tillich and all the great Protestants theologians because, in his heart of hearts, he sees them all as part of the same creation. Through his efforts, or the world's efforts, that unity cannot be taken away. I think one of his great lines was, "We don't have to become 'one.' We're already one. We just have to free ourselves of the illusion that we are not."

To be a religious person is not to figure out how I'm different from anybody else and special and chosen and unique and better, but how I'm part of the same creation that God made, that everyone belongs to. This is a more unifying source of interfaith dialogue than these identity quests that are always asking, "How am I different? How am I better? How am I unique? What do I know that they don't know?" From Merton's point of view these kinds of identity quests lead to division and become one of the great vehicles of evil in the twentieth century. People don't hurt one another because they want to be equal, it's more because they want to be special and feel they are better. That's the thing that has to be overcome through nonviolence, through dialogue, and through self-reflection.

I don't think happiness was a big goal for Merton. Happiness is a small byproduct of high aspirations. If happiness comes with truth, then Merton would take happiness, but if sadness comes with truth, if despair comes with truth, then he thought it is our responsibility to honor those things too.

He got a letter from a man who was writing a book on success. He was querying all these successful people and asking them how they became successes in America. He sent Merton a letter asking, "How did you become this successful monk?" Merton wrote him back in a letter, "I don't consider myself a success and I don't think success is something anybody should aspire to. I would tell people be anything. Be crazy. Be a drunk. Be a loser, but avoid success like the plague. The only reason you're probably writing to me is because my book was a bestseller. Had I to do it over again I would not make that same mistake. I wouldn't write a best-selling book. Success is living death." Now he didn't say that exactly—I'm paraphrasing—but that was the essence of what he wrote back. The problem with success isn't that you're successful. It's that you begin thinking of yourself as a "success." You develop a sense of superiority, a sense of not only being better than other people but independent of the general human suffering. So then you take it upon yourself to improve others or to tell them how "you made" yourself successful, which in effect separates you from being in solidarity with other people in their suffering. So that's why Merton thought that the concept of success, or thinking of yourself as successful, was anathema to the spiritual life. It is a winner/loser sense of yourself, which is not what a monk is. A monk, if anything, is somebody who chooses to be on the side of the losers or at least to be on the side of humanity.

Now happiness, I think, is probably similar to success. One of the great things Martin Luther King ever said was, "A person has not started living until they cease identifying with their own personal problems and begin identifying with the problems of all humanity." Those are pretty high stakes. If you identify with the problems of all humanity, you're not going to be conventionally happy, because humanity is not conventionally happy, and certainly not conventionally contented. Look at Martin Luther King's life—a life of bravery, sacrifice, and to some extent, martyrdom. That is a responsible life. Of course I don't know about Martin Luther King's inner life in terms of whether he felt happiness in what he was doing or if there was a deeper joy. I know that the "Mountain Top" speech gives us an indication of the responsibilities and the inner heights of a prophet.

There's an Old Testament tradition about how one tells a true prophet from a false prophet. In the Old Testament a true prophet is usually somebody who does not bring good news. And a prophet usually brings an alternative, "We can go this way or we can go this way, your choice." False prophets usually give you an answer, a direction. In that sense Merton meets the test. He told us who we were. Another test of a true prophet in the Old Testament is that he is usually hurt by his calling. He suffers for being a prophet. He doesn't benefit; he doesn't make money from being a prophet. Certainly Merton didn't suffer like Martin Luther King, but there is a sense where he definitely didn't profit, and he certainly didn't become rich or famous from his prophecies, so he meets that test. A third test of the true prophet is that he challenges us rather than makes us feel good about ourselves. The false prophet is somebody who tells us that we're great the way we are. The true prophet is somebody who says, "We need to take another look." In that sense Merton certainly fit the bill as a contemplative culture critic.

The Natural World

Nature was another deep and abiding consolation for Merton. In his early years at the monastery he rarely was allowed access to the woods surrounding Gethsemani. His joy when the restrictions were eased is palpable. Many of the observations regarding the forest, sky, and animals rival his reverent accounts of traditional worship.

∂ৎ ∂ৎ ∂ৎ

Kathleen Deignan: Merton was born into a family that was awake and alive to nature. He was after all a landscape painter's son. The fact of his being born to artists—his mother Ruth had studied interior design in Paris—provided his early education on being present to nature, beholding it in silence, observing it, being with it. His father Owen especially tutored him in the art of beholding. Merton accompanied his father on many of Owen's landscape painting adventures and outings. His father taught him to be open and look deeply at the natural world, and to celebrate his seeing. Merton has a very disciplined way of looking at the world. He is born into a certain kind of sensibility where the natural world is sensed as sacred. While his parents were not religious practitioners, they were engaged in reverencing nature. This deep beholding of nature became an early way of prayer for Merton and what Christians call a way of natural contemplation.

Merton had a Franciscan soul. Saint Francis of Assisi is the embodiment of a human being engaged in a celebratory, familial intimacy with nature and the natural world. Something of Francis's spirit spoke to Merton in the urban environment of Columbia University in New York as he read the writings of St. Bonaventure and other Franciscan writers. From them Merton discovers a sacramental way of understanding the world, of understanding creation as the embodiment, so to speak, of divinity. At Columbia Merton enthusiastically read William Blake and a host of writers who viewed the natural world as numinous and as epiphanies of the sacred. He borrows a notion of the "inscape" of things from Gerard Manley Hopkins, the English Jesuit, that each created thing has its particular form that can be apprehended as vibrant, dynamic, and emitting a numinous spirit life, almost as if everything had its own subjectivity.

If Merton had a Franciscan soul, he had a Cistercian heart. The Cistercian tradition that Merton encountered at the Abbey of Gethsemani was deeply contemplative. Saint Bernard of Clairvaux, though not the founder but really the father of the Cistercian movement, invited contemplatives to live in a profound simplicity with the natural world. Cistercians always chose valleys for the establishment of their early monasteries, simple places, humble places, so that the contemplative, the monk, could awaken to the vibrancy of the spirit of God in the natural world. This is what Merton discovered at Gethsemani. Monks celebrate in their liturgies the cycles of nature. A monk lives with a certain degree of intimacy with the natural world. So, whether it was the psalms of the Scriptures, or the psalms that seemed always to be arising out of Merton's own spirit as he communed with nature, Merton experienced profound states of intimate presence to Gethsemani's natural environment. In the 1950s Merton took the job of the abbey's forester, which afforded him new opportunities for solitude outside the monastic enclosure, now in the wider embrace of the forest itself and the woodlands around the monastery. He also at the time was reading Thoreau. He says in his journals that he aimed to become a competent naturalist.

Then in the 1960s Merton experienced new engagements with nature. He received permission to spend time in a hermitage built for him on one of Gethsemani's knobs. Here on Mount Olivet he experienced what I like to call his almost marrying the natural world, marrying the

forest. He speaks of the forest as his bride in his writings. It's such a beautiful way of understanding what was happening in his deep emotional life and mystical life. When he became a permanent hermit and lived alone day in and day out in the cycle of the seasons, he settled more deeply into the silence and mystery of nature. At the same time, in the 1960s he began reading books on Celtic spirituality and discovered, he said, something of his own true nature. He said that he began to understand what was driving him into the woods, and driving him to write and to be the poet that he was. He discovered this Celtic monk, so to speak, within himself.

There's a gorgeous little essay called "From Pilgrimage to Crusade" in the collection *Mystics and Zen Masters* where he describes in such an eloquent way his understanding of what these wild Celtic monks were up to in their abandonment of the social world to live on remote islands in the North Atlantic or on mountaintops. Merton understood that, as they set off out to sea in their little skin boats, these Celtic monks were in quest of their place of resurrection. Wherever those waves would take them, they believed, would be their place of resurrection. He identified with them, because he was, as he said of himself, a marginal person. Always looking for the boundaries or perimeters where somehow there was the ability to more deeply interface with that holy invisible, manifesting itself and becoming visible in the beauty of nature.

One of the turns for Merton, in relationship to his own nature/spirituality/creation mysticism, was the result of his exploration of the Zen tradition of Buddhism. Zen for Merton was a disciplined way of being present, a disciplined way of stilling and quieting the mind. Zen, he discovered, was a helpful and effective way of silencing one's afflictions, all of these noises in the head that can cause tremendous suffering and distraction. In Merton's later writings one begins to see a spareness in his verse. Merton's poetry becomes leaner as he describes the natural world.

Winter trail photo by Thomas Merton.

Merton found a hospice in the natural world, a marvelous refuge, a sanctuary for the healing of his own very, very complex nature. Part of the reason why Thomas Merton is so interesting is because of the complexity of his nature. He is so brilliant and yet at the same time he has a beautiful naiveté about life and about experience. We know that he has almost a compulsion to write. He cannot not write. One of my friends describes him as hypergraphic. And I think that in what he calls the utterly innocent speech of nature, in the variety of languages that nature spoke to him, Merton became quieter. It really did silence him. And I think that in listening to these exquisite other vocabularies, Merton was drawn out of himself, out of his own mind, out of his own inner conversations. Somehow in the woods he really did honor that vow of silence or that promise of silence that is so much a part of the Cistercian life. It seems that the natural world, the woods, his opportunities when he had them to travel in nature, really were a tremendous healing for him. Merton is most lighthearted, most buoyant and jubilant, when he's writing about nature. So, yes, I think for Merton the natural world is the ground of healing.

Merton believed that it was the vocation of human persons to be gardeners of paradise. Within nature Merton acquired a Celtic and Cistercian habit of heart of longing for paradise. For Merton paradise was not the other world or the next world; it was this world fully beheld, fully beloved. And so somehow some members of our species have to do that for the rest of us. It's as if some of us are ordained to keep festival and celebrate life by their attention to the natural world. Merton's words of celebration are available to me and become a way for me as an urbanite and New Yorker, as a person in my hurried and harried world, to see through the eyes of someone who allowed his senses to open, and allowed his senses to become still, and distilled the beauty that awaits me if I care to slow down and to look and to listen and to taste and to touch and to smell. So I think that Merton is inviting us, as he does in so many things, to come to life in relationship to the nature which is our greater self. I don't have the woodlands of Kentucky to visit each day but I do have trees. I have tree-lined streets. I have houseplants that I wake up to every morning and somehow, as I offer them something of nourishment, they offer me something of nourishment and they teach me how to be faithful to turning to the sun, of how to move through seasons, of dying and being fallow and coming to life again. All these things in the smallest and tiniest places reveal the natural world's great wisdom to us. In the natural world revealing itself to us is great wisdom.

One of the things I love most about Merton is the way he invites his readers into a central mystery of the Christian tradition, which is the mystery of the Incarnation. We celebrate that mystery most explicitly in the revelation of Christ, and we say the most wonderfully paradox things about this embodiment of divinity in this human person. All through our tradition Jesus is the central icon, the central sacrament, if you will, of this mystery of divinity's embodiment in nature. But as we have spent these thousands of years, these several millennia, reflecting on this great mystery of the Incarnation, we've come to understand the divinity is dwelling in the cosmos itself. Merton really understood this. He helps us recover one of the most, I think, important elements of our Christian tradition, our Catholic Christian tradition especially, in this practice of what is called natural contemplation.

As spiritual masters began to deepen their understanding of an explicitly Christian way of being human and explored paths to embody a sense of the sacred and the revelation that Christians had received, they began to articulate various pathways by which a human person could have the experience of transformation into Christ. And one of the ways, one of the first ways, they developed was to teach the senses to behold what someone like St. Bonaventure, following St. Augustine, would call the "vestiges of God" in creation, the vestiges of the Creator, the footprints of God in the natural world. And then to follow those footprints, as Bonaventure would say, back to their source. This Bonaventuran tradition deeply influenced Merton, the great celebration of divinity manifesting itself in the myriad of forms, in what we call in the Christian tradition the *cataphatic* forms of divinity expressing its own creativity, of God manifesting God's creativity in the world.

This, of course, is the ground of our sacramental spirituality as Christians. We are people who take incarnation seriously. For Christians life is sacred—all life is sacred—because life is, as Merton might say, the very liturgy of God's own self. Life embodies in the myriad forms what no one form could ever perfectly express of God's infinite wonder and diversity and creativity. This is a very important feature and facet of Merton's teaching right now, when we realize that our natural world is in such jeopardy because of our failure to see its sacrality, of our not beholding nature in a sacred manner. It seems most urgent right now that the Christian tradition recover something of its rich legacy in this form of natural contemplation that celebrates and teaches us clearly that we are to be, as Merton said, these celebrants of the natural world, while we have this world to celebrate.

Paul Quenon: Being out in the midst of nature was a very important part of Merton's prayer life. That was quite obvious. It was part of the monastic routine to go out in the woods and do some work, or out in the fields. Everybody did that but he had a special appreciation of it. So he would go outside and read. Everybody would read in the garden during the summertime. Sometimes we would be going out on a truck to a distant field to pick up hay or something and he would come along with a book, leave the crew, go into the woods, and read a book. He did this for two reasons; one was to witness to the fact that work is not everything. Also it gave him a chance to get into a different environment, you know, at a distance.

Not everybody appreciated that. I remember one of the professed brothers was saying, "Well, that bum. Here we were doing all this work and he goes off with a book." One time he told us that after Mass it's good just to go outdoors and cleanse your senses and listen to the breeze in the trees.

He loved the cats. He liked the cats better than dogs. He thought people like dogs because they jump all over you and give you a lot of attention, whereas a cat is much more self-possessed, and that's what he liked about the cat. He said the cat was a much more spiritual animal.

Monica Weis: One of the things that Merton was very concerned about when he was making his decision to go to the Trappist monastery was whether or not he could let go of what might be called his Franciscan heart, because he loved nature and wasn't so sure that he could give up everything. His journals tell us that not too long after being there in the monastery and going through the ritual day by day he discovers that for monks it's not an either/or but it's a both/and experience. He talked about nature being very much part of his prayer and that he had no scruples about it. That's a really meaningful moment, because nature is starting to make him whole. It's starting to bring his whole person into oneness and a unity. The first time I read the seven volumes of his journals I kept noticing a curious facet of them: "Why all these weather reports? What's going on with this man?" It isn't until the 1960s, and I think it's even an Ash Wednesday entry, that Merton finally wrote: "The weather is very important to me. I need to mention it. It is part of me and a day on which I do not notice the weather is a day on which I am not all together." So I see that recognition as a beginning of some transformation that's taking place and deepening him as a spiritual writer, as a priest and as a Trappist, that's deepening him as a human being.

Another thing I noticed reading the journals is that very often Merton will be writing about nature and making a wonderful description of, let's say, the sunlight over the hills as he's standing at the kitchen door after night prayer looking out. Suddenly his description of nature will just move into a prayer such as, "Oh, God, lock my heart onto You." I would ask myself, "Wait a minute. How did we get there? Where does that come from?" At other times he might be writing seriously about prayer and contemplation, or the results of his meditation, and he will suddenly employ a nature metaphor. And then sometimes the inner and the outer experiences merge, and his writing goes back and forth between nature and prayer. It's as if the internal and external landscape are all one.

It reminds me very much of the poet Walt Whitman, who was always talking about the issue of "merging." For Whitman the spiritual and the material are all one. I think Thomas Merton had some of that. I recently saw a card with a Merton quote: "Each breath we take is a gift. Each moment of life is a grace." It goes back to his love for William Blake. One of Blake's famous lines is "All that is, is holy." Merton used that line as a chapter heading in *Seeds of Contemplation*. Blake's view was part of Merton's interior life.

Solitude

It has been said by many that Merton found in solitude the ground for his greatest consolation. The crowded, busy community that was Gethsemani presented a tension that endured through his life there. His journals reflect his frustration with solitude's absence and deep, profound joy when he was able to avail himself of it. I've never read anyone who made being sick with the flu in the infirmary sound more sublime. Merton writes of convalescing in solitude with the fervor you might find in someone's description of their first trip to Paris. Illustrating his love of solitude was a challenge. True, there are many examples in his writing extolling solitude, but how does one photograph it?

The shed in the woods that Merton christened St. Ann's was one of his first opportunities at the monastery to spend long periods in solitude. One of the monks was kind enough to point it out to me. It became my "base camp" as I sought a way to bring Merton's solitude to life. I spent hours walking around St. Ann's trying to imagine what Merton might have seen or heard. I stood inside for a bit even though most of the floor is now rotted away. Fear of snakes and lack of a place to sit got me back outside before long. I gained a lot from my time at St. Ann's, including a remarkable variety of chigger bites. I can't recall Merton mentioning this, but I can attest that if you spend any time in St. Ann's wood without bug repellent, you will know fully the wonder of God's little creatures for many days after. On a slightly more elevated plane, I also tasted some of the pleasure of simply sitting for hours, quiet, unattached to anything but the creation around me.

John Eudes Bamberger: Merton had a very strong and very deep need for solitude. When he was still in high school in England, he would go off by himself for a large part of the day and spend it alone. When he was a professor at St. Bonaventure College, he spent a great deal of his free time alone.

Merton's need for solitude was not so much an evasion as it was a communion, a communing with life at a level where it spoke to him most personally. So his need for solitude was very real and very personal. On the other hand, in my opinion, he also needed people, and that was his struggle. After he was in solitude for a certain time at Gethsemani, he began having too many visitors, in my opinion. I think that's what got him into difficulties with staying at Gethsemani. That's when he began to be dissatisfied with hermit life at Gethsemani, because he had allowed too many visitors to come. If someone needed or expected something from Merton, his tendency was to go along. He liked people. He liked to keep them happy. He liked to please them, and that was also deep in him. At the same time he'd be very frustrated. No doubt it surprises many of the people who visited him and thought he was having a great time to realize, reading his journals, that underneath he was wishing they'd go home. So this is one aspect of the picture of his hermit years, the years he spent in his hermitage full time from 1965 to 1968. These years were very fruitful and meant a great deal to him. They made a serious contribution to his life of prayer, to his growth in spirit, but they also left him vulnerable.

Michael Mott: The whole question of Merton wanting a hermitage and wanting to be a hermit is fascinating. The hermit theme is present all

the way through Merton's work. In the beginning he's asking for solitude, for contemplation. Really what he's asking for is privacy, a few hours of privacy, and in a monastery with three hundred souls, that's not easy to get. I bring that up immediately because it is the hermit sign. Merton himself got very angry with people saying you should develop a hermitage within, an imaginary hermitage into which you can retreat, that you don't need a physical hermitage. But, for all that, he constantly reminds activists, particularly political activists, there's a contemplative side that's got to be cherished and nourished, especially among activists. He does this to the Berrigans and he does it with others. If you are simply an activist, you're like a dragon chasing its own tail and chewing on its own tail. You act for the sake of activity and you don't act for any good. You've got to—like Christ—you've got to get up on the mountain, and spend time on the mountain getting yourself together, and then you go down and reengage. Now there is the idea of the hermitage within, and it's got to be honored, and Merton would say that everyone should have their "inner hermitage." We all need to honor our contemplative side. But Merton also needed and wanted a physical hermitage. First it was a garden shed pulled into the woods that he called Saint Ann's. Then he finally gets his own concrete block hermitage on Mount Olivet. And we must not forget that he earned that hermitage. He had worked in the community for over twenty years before he was allowed by his abbot even to spend the night in the hermitage.

Lawrence Cunningham: Being a hermit is a very old tradition in monasticism. It goes all the way back to the desert fathers and mothers of the late third and early fourth centuries. After a monk has led a disciplined life in the monastery, he or she may retire to the eremitical life, to the life of the hermit, for greater prayer and greater reflection. The Cistercians, the Trappists, never had a tradition of this, or they had a very

St. Ann's Hermitage at Gethsemani is slowly rotting in the woods near the monastery. I wondered if something shouldn't be done to preserve it. I've not heard much interest in or support for the idea.

thin tradition of this, and so Merton was really the first monk to manage to break this mold. He was a mold breaker in that sense. And Merton's argument was that he wanted to have more time for solitude, more time for meditation, more time for writing really serious stuff. He did not think that becoming solitary meant becoming lonely, or hating the world. He said, "You know, I've gone to the hermitage not because I hate the world. I go to the hermitage to deepen my consciousness, to be more in communion with the world."

Merton was a restless soul. After a year or two in the hermitage he begins scheming about how he could travel. So there's always that kind of ambivalence in him. He does try to lead a hermit's life. He exercises fidelity to its demands. We know from letters he writes, and from his hermitage journals, that, even though he was living alone, he was getting up at 2 o'clock in the morning. He was praying and meditating. He was doing manual labor, devoting himself to literary work. The life of a hermit is a rare phenomenon in the Catholic Church, but it is seen in the monastic tradition, as it is by the way in Buddhism, as a natural progression of someone who has been faithful to community life as a monk.

Kathleen Deignan: I think I've only been to Gethsemani twice in my life, and of course as a student of Merton, as a disciple of Merton, it has been a wonderful opportunity for me to make a pilgrimage to what is, for me, a sacred space. It was in his hermitage that he wrote so many of the words that inspired me and so many others. It's easy to imagine Merton in his hermitage when you are visiting it, as you move through its small rooms. I imagine Merton on that porch of his through the many hours of the day as the natural world was changing and beckoning him to observe something of its beauty. In my mind's eye I can place Merton in that small chapel where he celebrated Eucharist.

But in fact one doesn't have to use one's imagination. Merton's own words from his hermitage vividly let you know what he was experiencing or witnessing or beholding there. He spoke of what a day in his hermitage was like in an essay he wrote, "Day of a Stranger." Describing his hermit's day, he writes of his presence to the natural world, to the creatures surrounding his hermitage that he came to know so intimately. He knew the communities of birds all around him. He writes of his familiarity with other "presences" and "spirits." He wrote that the teeming heart of living families were present to him in his hermitage and shared his hermitage's small knob, a way of describing his own heart, in a sense. His heart was larger and spoke to a greater body than only this community of the natural world. His heart spoke with the poets he was reading, with the psalmist of the sacred songs he read or sang every day, pouring, as he said, his psalms out all over the country of his tiny neighborhood, of the world of persons whom he had known and loved.

The hermitage and the circumference of his hermitage world, however wide that was, became a neighborhood full of familiars he encountered as he walked and explored its boundaries. His hermit's neighborhood was full of people of the spirit, people whom he was being inspired by in his reading. It was full of the saints that he walked with in the dailiness of the liturgical life. What I love about reading Merton's nature writings is that he begins, perhaps, by telling you something about the weather, but soon you're reflecting on the liturgy of the day, and that is taking him then to some sort of deeper decision to be more mindful, or to be more devoted, or to be more awake or alive. There's a wonderful, wonderful sweep in the way that his beginning prayer in nature brings him to the most concrete and specific decisions to be more profoundly human. To be more profoundly a communicant in what he calls the present festival. It's a wonderful invitation to all of us really.

Paul Quenon: It was practically unknown in modern times for a Cistercian to become a hermit. The only instances were people who might have been in the monastery and then left. We had one hermit when I came to Gethsemani in 1958. His name was Herman Hanekamp, a good name for a hermit. He had been in temporary vows and then left and moved about two miles west of here. He had a little piece of property and built himself a hermitage and lived with goats in the house. He had a big white beard and would go walking down to Culvertown for his groceries. He would walk to the monastery for Mass every day. Kind of a character, but I think Fr. Louis admired him very much. He died in 1958 and is buried in our cemetery.

I believe there was somebody else from Gethsemani in Canada who had become a hermit, but it really wasn't until the 1960s that legislation was changed in our constitutions so that a Cistercian could become a hermit. And a lot of that was simply because Merton was pushing to become a hermit himself. Dom James wanted to keep him here at Gethsemani, and actually Dom James himself wanted to be a hermit, but nobody knew that. So Dom James was highly instrumental in putting the legislation through the General Chapter to allow for hermits in our Order. There was, of course, an ideal of hermit life which was broadly accepted among monks, and, of course, the Rule of St. Benedict allows a monk to leave after many years in the monastery and fight the devil in solitary battle out in the wilderness. Well, Dom James asked the General Chapter, why weren't we observing the Rule of St. Benedict on that score?

Prior to this formal change in the constitutions, Dom James was simply following the form of Cistercian life when he was denying Merton's early requests to become a hermit. The abbot didn't have much of a choice as he had to adhere to our constitutions. Either that or change the rules of the Order, which is eventually what he did or helped to do.

When a person becomes a hermit he has to be beyond any need to justify himself. In a sense he can't really explain to anybody, maybe not even to himself, why he is a hermit. It's based on a call from God to enter into this solitude, which is a deeper kind of intimacy with Christ. And maybe he'll get out there in solitude and find out it's not all that intimate, but God still wants him to be there. It's a mystery why it is, of why this happens in the church, but it has happened in the church for centuries and it's really a special thing for people to be called to that. Not everybody who tries it can do it. I'm not sure if Fr. Louis ultimately could have done it. He only had three years to try, and that's nothing like living out a hermit's life for fifteen or twenty years, the way our Fr. Roman has done, Gethsemani's current hermit. I do think Fr. Louis was genuinely called to the eremitical life. I wonder if he had the ability to live the eremitical life ultimately. I think God gave him that call so that the rest of us would be inspired, so that there would be kind of an outbreak of a new dimension within our Order and way of life. So, now, because of Merton and Dom James, we do have hermits. It is an option.

It's not as popular as it was, say, fifteen or twenty years ago. The new generation of monks is not on a quest to build hermitages. So it may have been a wave of enthusiasm that has temporarily waned but that will come back again sometime, and we won't have to go through the agony and gymnastics to get it the way we did in Merton's generation.

In his quest for a more solitary life, Merton was a voice in his own generation. His was a voice of somebody who marched to a different drummer. We've had this already in our American tradition, the pre–Civil War writers who were great individualists. We always need some people like that.

Every generation should have solitaries. Hilaire Belloc said that the mark of a healthy civilization is that it has hermits. It seems like a paradox but it's true. Societies need people who can stand outside the system and look at it from a different perspective. I think Merton did that. The unique thing about Merton, as opposed to Thoreau or Emily Dickinson, was that he was consciously coming out of the church's desert tradition. He studied the Desert Fathers. He was reaching much farther back than other Americans who valued solitude. Merton was able to bring a very deep and rich tradition to the present situation and reevaluate it. The falseness of the ideals and the tastes of people in our culture become much more evident when they are held up against the deep spiritual values of the Desert Fathers. I know that people don't know what to make of Merton's desire to be a hermit and I think they never will because . . . well, I won't go on about that.

Elena Malits: When Merton wrote about himself as a hermit, living in solitude, he wrote about the inevitable struggle and the doubts that come with living alone. I think that this is a kind of experience that we would all recognize when perhaps we have to make an important decision and we're scared to death of having to face the crisis of making that decision. So we put it off by busyness. Merton believed that silence and solitude inevitably will make us face up to reality. The more we talk, the more we run around and do things, the easier it is to put off facing those things none of us really want to face. Many great revolutionaries spent some time in jail. Think of Gandhi; think of Martin Luther King Jr. That time in jail was a time when they were cut off from their ordinary activities, where the necessity of looking at themselves and what they are doing takes over. I think that's what Merton thought solitude did for him. When you experience that kind of thing, it's hardly a sweet and happy illumination. I mean it's as hard as life can get—to question who you are and what you think you're doing and whether that is really what God wants or not, and all of those doubts about one's own rectitude, righteousness, being on the right track, come up and become difficult in solitude. I don't know that there's any way around those "epiphanies" about yourself in solitude. You just have to live through it.

Anthony Padovano: I think the hermitage represented for Merton something he always wanted. There are two kinds of monastic life in Catholicism: the eremitical, in which you live in much solitude, and the cenobitical, in which you live in community. Merton went to the Cistercian life, which is a community life. You pray together, you eat together, work together. Merton, however, was always attracted to the Camaldolese and the Carthusians. He was always looking for more solitude. I remember his abbot, James Fox, telling me at one point: "I tried to settle it by making him a forester so he could spend a lot of time up in some forest lookout checking for forest fires. So he'd have a lot of time away from the community on his own." So I think Merton's eventually having his hermitage was not as discontinuous with his previous life as it seemed. In fact, if you read Merton carefully, all the things he later became were there in the beginning. His hermitage was a retreat of sorts. He was afraid that he was too much with the world and too much with the monastery. Solitude in a hermitage did help him to some extent, but he kept wandering out of it because he really, I don't think, was meant to be a hermit. He was meant to be connected. The hermitage wound up being more of a partial solution to his problems. He wound up inviting people out there, having dinner with them, giving retreats there. These things were not what you strictly mean by leading an eremitical life.

Paul Pearson: Was Merton a conventional hermit? Well, I don't think there ever was anything such as a conventional hermit. You know, Merton was breaking with recent tradition within the Catholic Church. Certainly within the Cistercian Order there had been hermits in the early days of the Order, and they had really been forgotten about. As Merton was pushing for reintroducing hermits in the monastic life, for being allowed to live as a hermit himself, he really had to justify that from the tradition. When Dom James came to defend his position, and get permission from the General Chapter for Merton to live as a hermit, it was because he had allowed Merton the opportunity to explore the sources of the Order and to find that there was a tradition there for hermits. But, what is your traditional hermit? Gregory Zilboorg's criticism of Merton, when he told Merton in an interview that he wanted to have a hermitage on Times Square, really, I think, gets to the core of Merton. There is this great attraction to the solitary life, but he was also somebody who needed that contact with other people. How do you define what a hermit is? There's no one definition.

In the days of Julian of Norwich you would get people who would be walled up in a small cell beside the church where meals would be passed in to them. They would spend their life in prayer. That would be one definition of being a hermit, being a solitary, but there are other definitions. I think Merton was in the process of discovering a definition of being a hermit, being a solitary, that was appropriate *for him*. Certainly in 1968, as he was exploring other places where Gethsemani might set up some hermitages, I think he speaks a bit about finding that kind of balance, possibly being a solitary for six months a year, having more involvement with the community and other things for the other six months. I think that was who he was. I think that in some ways makes the hermit life more understandable for people. It's not just another matter of turning your back on the world and having nothing whatsoever to do with the world. The hermit life is, as Merton saw it, a vocation *for* the world, and that was the way it would have played out for him if he had been at it longer.

So was he a successful hermit? What's a successful hermit? I think it was what he needed. I think it was something that his community and the church needed as well. You need a whole range of different religious possibilities. That's part of the universal nature of the church. It's made up of a very diverse group of people who are somehow part of one community.

Monica Weis: In my judgment Merton's writing did not take "another step" once he became a hermit. I find that his writing and his spirituality changed once he was given permission in the late 1940s to spend time outside the confines of the traditional cloister grounds at Gethsemani. It's the silence and the solitude he found being in nature that expanded his heart. And it's the solitude he found in Gethsemani's natural environment that kept his heart expanding. In his later years, when he had more time to write at the hermitage, he had more solitude and so perhaps was being—I don't even want to use the word "productive," "being more productive in his writing" sounds terrible. Perhaps he was more "productive" in his prayer. So let's change that word to "fruitful": in the hermitage he was more fruitful in his writing and in his prayer. I don't see the time in the hermitage making a right angle change in his writing, but just a continuing blossoming.

View from St. Ann's hermitage.

Christine Bochen: Questioning the role of a hermit is interesting because it leads in two, possibly three, directions. First what is the hermit's role as experienced by the hermit? Then what is the relationship between the hermit and the community? And finally what does the hermit have to say to the rest of us who are not going to become hermits? Merton was very drawn to a life of solitude, and in reading his journals one wonders whether that might have been what surprised him most about monastic life at Gethsemani. He initially thought there would be more of an opportunity to experience solitude by entering the monastery, but Gethsemani became a very crowded monastery in the late 1940s. So Merton, as his life at Gethsemani went on, was ever hungry for a deeper solitude, and the hermit life afforded him that opportunity for an experience of deeper solitude. It meant that he lived by himself, now still on the grounds of the monastery, still participating on occasion in the worship and the prayer of the community, but for the most part enjoying that experience of quiet that he so longed for during the course of his life.

The role of the hermit, it seems to the rest of us, is someone who points to a dimension of life about which the rest of us are often unmindful. By the radical choice to live a life of solitude as a hermit, the hermit is inviting others of us to taste something of a life of quiet. One of my favorite Merton essays is "Creative Silence," a piece he wrote for the *Bloomin' Newman* at the University of Kentucky. In that essay he talks about how we live a busy-busy existence, and how the contemplative, and maybe in this context we can think about the hermit as an intense kind of contemplative, has a way of reminding us that there's another dimension beyond this superficial, busy-busy existence. And so the hermit is a symbol. The hermit is a reminder. The hermit is something of an invitation to explore in ourselves a way of being, a dimension of being, or a dimension of living that we so easily ignore.

I sometimes ask my students whether they think that the hermit life is an escape. They become very thoughtful and say, "Probably, yes it is." We talk about it a bit and reflect on the fact that it might be an escape or it might be another way of being present, a more mysterious and more paradoxical way of being present to the world. Is being a hermit about withdrawal? Well certainly, but it is also a form of engagement, and an engagement not only in the life of the spirit, but in a way of being present in the world that is and can be socially responsible.

Rosemary Radford Ruether was only one correspondent of Merton's who challenged his vocation as a monk. She thought he ought to get out of the monastery and march down the streets of Washington, DC where things needed to be done. But Merton knew he had another vocation. He glimpsed a value in another way of being, the value of a life of prayer and work in solitude, not only because it is a symbol or a communication with the rest of us about what might really matter, but because such a way of being present to life has a value in its own right. I think that the value of solitude is something that you either get or you don't, or you get a little bit and maybe need to work on the rest. Maybe this would be a very different kind of world if there were more hermits among us.

Part 3

Opening to the World

Revelations

*I*f one asks Merton admirers to name landmark incidents in his life, it's rare if "the 4th and Walnut revelation" is not included. This occurred in Louisville, Kentucky, in 1958, at the intersection of 4th Street, the city's most vibrant street at the time, and Walnut, a street that has since been renamed Muhammad Ali in honor of the community's famous native son. Merton was in Louisville for a doctor's appointment. He sees this great mix of people at 4th and Walnut and is overwhelmed by his sense of oneness with them. In his book Conjectures of a Guilty Bystander, *he uses the incident to express how he is changing from focusing on the concerns of the cloister to those of all the world. It's a beautiful piece of writing and it's little wonder that it has become a classic. Like his best work, it speaks to a wide variety of people on different levels. Recently the area has been renamed Thomas Merton Square. It's near the Catholic cathedral of Louisville. It's also right next to a thriving area of nightclubs and restaurants. My guess is Merton would enjoy the mix.*

The 4th and Walnut revelation confirmed for me that people become very protective of their interpretation of the Merton story. I intentionally did not include this incident in Soul Searching, *primarily because I had already done a version of it in* Gethsemani, *an earlier documentary I had produced on life at the monastery. In researching* Soul Searching *I had also talked with several scholars who, without discounting the significance of 4th and Walnut, pointed to earlier events in that decade which also signaled Merton's opening to the world.*

This photograph by Merton symbolizes for me his embrace of life outside the monastery walls (although I don't see 4th Street, and I'm pretty sure the trees aren't walnut).

Jonathan Montaldo, for example, says Merton becoming an American citizen in 1951 signals just as clearly that Merton was expanding his horizons. So it made sense to me to use some other way of showing this important development in Merton's spiritual journey.

This may have been a mistake. During the question and answer period of virtually every showing of Soul Searching I've done, people have questioned it being left out. For many it is akin to telling the story of Paul and leaving out a certain road trip to Damascus. I point out that Soul Searching shows other ways in which Merton is opening up to the world, but I can tell my explanation is falling on deaf ears.

Merton learned quickly that there were consequences when he did things that were not in keeping with prescribed expectations. People can have a decided ambivalence when spiritual models stray from the roles we have assigned them. I remember once being at the Abbey of Gethsemani at the same time as there was a conference of monks (male and female) from several different American Cistercian monasteries. They had a weeklong meeting in which they were sharing insights and challenges of their spiritual life. During this relatively rare occasion of inter-monastery collegiality, the conference participants scrupulously maintained their regular monastic schedule with one exception: during the midday meal they were allowed to interact as they ate rather than maintain the customary silence. I happened to walk through the dining area of one such meal and these exemplars of the monastic life were not only talking animatedly, in some cases they were even laughing! Well, I was scandalized.

I relate this in an intentionally over-the-top manner to underscore the absurdity of my reaction, but if I'm really honest I was initially, at the very least, surprised. Monks, at least my rigid conception of them at that time, just weren't supposed to relate to each other in this manner. Thankfully I immediately realized I was being ridiculous, but I also realized that this is the type of pigeonholing a monk and probably most professed religious endure. We have assigned them a very specific role or task and beware if they do anything else. So when Thomas Merton in the 1950s opened up to a wider worldview, several things happened.

His life was enriched emotionally and spiritually. He came into contact with diverse new friends and audiences. He blurred the sterile image many have of a monk. I wanted to convey these changes even as I detoured around 4th and Walnut.

Paul Pearson: Certainly when Thomas Merton entered Gethsemani in December, 1941, he was really turning his back on the world, shaking its dust off his feet. I think he imagined he'd have nothing further to do with the world. That comes across very, very strongly in some of the early poetry that he wrote at the monastery. He really speaks, not badly of the world, but his writing about the world in that poetry is very negative and even more so about cities and what men were doing in the world. Obviously this is 1941, with the war raging in Europe and the beginning of the war in the Far East.

In the early days of his conversion Merton was looking for this heavenly city, almost a mythical paradise that he saw as separate from the world. He equated the world with his own sin, with his own bad experiences in the world, and Cambridge, and so the monastery was a symbol of paradise for him. The central metaphors of *The Seven Storey Mountain* are inspired by Dante's *Divine Comedy*, the journey through hell and purgatory to paradise. In those first years in the monastery Merton portrayed Gethsemani as paradise, but he soon discovered that the world he thought he had left behind at the monastery gate in 1941 had followed him into the monastery. He was a human being, after all, and could not separate himself from the world. Gradually, however, he experiences a growing compassion for the world.

With the success of *The Seven Storey Mountain* people began writing to him, sharing their reactions to his autobiography and their problems with him, and Merton began to realize that he couldn't be separate from the world. Also, when he began teaching the younger monks in the monastery, he had to respond to them and to their problems. They

THOMAS MERTON (1915~68)

Trappist monk, poet, social critic, and spiritual writer. Born in Prades, France. After education at Cambridge, and Columbia Univ, he entered Abbey of Gethsemani, Trappist, Ky., 1941: ordained as priest, 1949. His autobiography *The Seven Storey Mountain* (1948), earned international acclaim. He is buried in abbey cemetery.

Presented by Thomas Merton Center Foundation

were coming from a very different world than earlier generations of monks. He had to work with them through their personal experiences of being monks of Gethsemani. Then, as he read deeply in preparation for his teaching conferences into the writings of the Desert Fathers, the great mystics and the Fathers of the church, he began to find a very different view of the world, a great deal more openness to the world than was certainly current in his thinking and in the thinking of a lot of those in the church at the time. This comes across clearly in his little book about Clement of Alexandria. He gives the impression with Clement that here was a man who could use what was best in the world of his time to teach people about Christ and what Christianity was truly about. In his reading of the Desert Fathers as well, he found that although they went out into the desert, the world followed them there.

In what could be considered Merton's sequel to his autobiography, *The Sign of Jonas*, he signals that his approach to the world had begun to change. In *Jonas* he writes that he had discovered that his "new desert" was compassion. He had been looking for the desert, that is, for more and more solitude, and yet he discovered through his work with the scholastics a very deep sense of compassion. He also wrote at one point in *Jonas*, "Your heart is my hermitage." He was already looking for a hermitage at that point. Yet he had this insight that compassion for another person could also lead him into a deeper solitude, but a solitude that resonated with the solitude within other people.

Merton's approach to the world gradually broadened through the later 1950s. References are often made to Merton's experience in Louisville at the corner of 4th and Walnut streets, but I don't think that was any great moment of conversion. It was no Damascus road. I think it was a moment of insight into what had already been happening within his life, and it just enabled him to express it in words. There are other instances where

The site of Merton's 4th and Walnut revelation has gone through a few changes over the years. 4th Street has become Fourth Street. Walnut Street has become Muhammad Ali Avenue, and the general area was recently renamed Thomas Merton Square. And all the people are still "shining like the sun."

Merton "opens to the world" in his writing, but they are often overlooked because people concentrate on the 4th and Walnut experience.

At the end of *The Sign of Jonas* Merton recorded being on the fire watch at the monastery, and people often consider it one of his greatest pieces of prose writing. He is writing in the early 1950s and his account of the fire watch is very introspective. As he goes through the different areas of the monastery, he's continually relating everything he sees to his own experience. But in *Conjectures of a Guilty Bystander* Merton recorded being on the fire watch for a second time in the early 1960s with a very different perspective. At one point he passes through the scriptorium, where the novices studied and kept their few personal things. The scriptorium no longer speaks to him of his own monastic life but of this new generation of novices. He says that Christ is as truly present in this room as upstairs in the chapel. It's a very strong affirmation of the presence of Christ among other people, as he said of his 4th and Walnut experience, when he saw people walking around "shining like the sun."

Jonathan Montaldo: Merton became an American citizen in 1951. He had held a British passport until then and thought, he said, that he didn't need an earthly passport to get into heaven. But in 1951 he decided to become an American citizen and he wrote that his becoming a citizen meant that he was accepting Gethsemani as it was and America as it was and himself as he was. He thought that the women at the Office of Naturalization and Immigration in downtown Louisville were going to get him into heaven. He was finally incarnating himself in America. It's exactly the same insight that he has at 4th and Walnut streets in 1958: "I love all these people, and we can't be strangers to one another." So while 4th and Walnut is an important moment in Merton's literary career, he personally had already discovered a sense of solidarity with the world. That solidarity wasn't as realized when he entered the monastery in search of solitude, but eventually the fruit of his real solitude at Gethsemani was his growing sense of compassion for everyone else.

Michael Mott: A time came when Merton began to open more to the world. For me a key symbolic work of this opening is his prose poem "Hagia Sophia." Sophia is divine wisdom but in the form of a young Jewish woman. Curiously enough, in the original journal record of that vision at 4th and Walnut in Louisville, he's really looking at the girls in Louisville. Then, when he goes to Lexington to see his friend, the painter Victor Hammer, Merton finds what is to him a portrait of the woman he's been seeing in his dreams and maybe seeing in the streets of Louisville. Incidentally she looks almost exactly the same as his nurse in 1966. It's really haunting, quite remarkable. No wonder he sat up and took notice when the nurse came in the room.

So is he just moving out into the world of women? In a sense, yes. It's women who bring Thomas Merton out into the world. It's not just the Hagia Sophia figure. It is also Julian of Norwich. It is also his correspondence with the poet Sister Mary Madeleva at Saint Mary's College in Indiana. He begins to ask himself, "What is being left out?" And so often he says, "Women have been left out. Women have been left out of the Church." And when his friend Mary Luke Tobin is going off to be one of a handful of female auditors at Vatican II, he says that women have been left out of the Roman Catholic Church, with a notable exception of Our Lady, for quite a long time, and it might be quite good if they got back in again.

Correspondence

One of the factors that contributed significantly to Merton's opening to the world was his increased exposure to people outside the monastery's walls via correspondence. I enjoyed the vivid image Michael Mott created in describing how Merton must have been like a "mad woodpecker" tapping out as many as twenty letters a day sometimes. Mott spoke for many Merton scholars when he told me it was fortunate that there wasn't e-mail in Merton's day or we wouldn't have the rich paper trail he left with his correspondence. Other scholars sniffed that the often technophobic monk would not have used a computer. My guess is that one of his young correspondents would've broken through Merton's initial misgivings and gotten him very enthused about the possibilities of e-mail and off he would've soared into cyberspace.

James Conner: When I entered the monastery, the practice was that a monk could only write and receive mail four times a year. The mail was both sent out and received open. And since a monk received mail only four times a year, it was the prior's job to go through the mail to see if there was something important that the monk needed to know prior to the next major feast day. So your mail was always read by someone else. Originally it was the abbot himself who would read the mail. Dom Frederick Dunne would spend hours, even though the community was much smaller at that time, trying to cull all the mail, both incoming and outgoing. The outgoing mail also had to be handed in, still open, and dropped in the abbot's box.

Jonathan Montaldo: The Thomas Merton Center at Bellarmine University in Louisville has over ten thousand pieces of Merton's correspondence that consists of Merton's letters to a correspondent, not their letters to him. These letters were to popes, Nobel Prize winners, poets, and ordinary people who wrote him, nuns, priests, and even nine-year-old kids. There's a whole collection of Merton's letters to a teenager, a California high school student who was editing her school's newspaper. The extant of Merton's correspondence is amazing, but also his willingness to correspond with a range of people, at length and not just brief notes, all the while writing his books and magazine articles, and continuing to follow the monastic schedule at Gethsemani through it all. From 1955 to 1965 Merton is the novice master, the person instructing and responsible for the new people who are coming to Gethsemani, and yet he takes time to write all these letters. These letters are a sign of

Merton's growing compassion for the world. One of the last books he prepared for publication before his death was a selection from his private journals called *A Vow of Conversation*. A vow of conversation! He conversed with people. He shared their problems. He made himself open to them.

There was certainly a segment of his correspondence with people like Erich Fromm, D. T. Suzuki, Boris Pasternak, and Latin American poets, that fulfilled Merton's need for connection with kindred spirits: writers, people interested in social issues and the problems of the day. Merton needed their input. After all, most of his news about current events was all secondhand, from magazine articles where events would be reported after the fact. But letter writing allowed him to stay in touch. So he was networking in the modern sense of the word with kindred spirits. This does not explain, however, why Merton wrote to kids and people asking for his spiritual advice, total strangers, in often long, seriously reflected letters. Such letters were expressions of Merton's compassion, his charity, certainly not just evidence of a need to connect. He enjoyed his connections with ordinary folks. He was a very sensitive person who really loved people.

Michael Mott: His correspondence was his vast web of friendship, taking in Pasternak in Russia, taking in the Sufis, taking in a great many other people. I mean, anybody who says that Thomas Merton was this monk in a closed order isolated in the middle of Kentucky is out of their mind. I don't know many people who have a web of correspondence that anywhere near matches his in its range and in his fascination with all kinds of subjects. It's part of his mission. He's writing letters to people who are in trouble. The interesting thing about it is, however, that he never takes over somebody else's spiritual journey or takes it from them. Merton always refers things back to the person writing him: "I think you had better explore this and that and the other thing, you seem to be leaning in this direction." That's as far as he goes, showing respect for the other person, knowing it's the other person that makes the decision.

The fascination of this whole thing is heaven knows what would have happened to any of us scholars of Merton if the man had had e-mail. What a nightmare that would've been! He sat there at a manual typewriter pecking away with one or two fingers. He must have been like a mad woodpecker. I mean twenty letters a day was not unusual. I don't say he sent out twenty letters every day, but twenty letters in a day was not unusual with him. And pretty full letters, too. They weren't little bits and pieces, you know, "Great to hear from you, Hank. I'll get back to you when I have the time." He was a phenomenal letter writer.

William Shannon: After the success of *The Seven Storey Mountain*, Merton received a lot of fan mail that could be answered with a thank-you note, but eventually he began getting people opening themselves to him and asking for advice. He really became a spiritual director through these letters that he wrote to these people. These letters put him in touch with people outside the monastery who kept him informed about what was going on in the world, but also his letters to them gave him a freedom to write what he really wanted to say, because his published writings were censored by other monks of his Order, who often had a very strict sense of what was proper for a monk to write.

A few years ago I read the book At Home in the World *edited by Mary Tardiff, OP, which presents the extensive correspondence Merton had with Rosemary Radford Ruether. At first glance this seemed like an unlikely pairing, a middle-aged cloistered monk and a young feminist theologian. I found their exchange fascinating and was pleased when Dr. Ruether agreed to an interview at her southern California home.*

Rosemary Ruether: When I wrote my first book, *The Church Against Itself*, I was a relative youngster in my twenties. I was interested in getting some kind of feedback from Catholic theologians. Amusingly enough, I thought first of sending it to Fulton Sheen. That turned out to be quite absurd. He was totally uninterested. I got a secretarial letter claiming that I just wanted his autograph. I sent the book to Merton and Merton immediately responded and was very interested in it and gave me feedback. Merton immediately responded to my book as a peer. And he began to address the issues of my book on a kind of level that spoke to me as if I were his intellectual peer. That was in the mid-1960s, a time when the official Catholic world didn't treat women equally, not that they do now, they did even less then. In fact the responses to my book from some were very patronizing: "Imagine, her thinking she has something to say." I sent my book to Merton on a kind of hope and got a good answer. So essentially my correspondence with him grew out of that quest to get someone to read it and give me feedback, not simply to judge its literary capacity but to look at it more as a theologian.

I had moved from finishing my doctorate to teaching at Howard University School of Religion, which was a black seminary, and I was working in the inner city in Washington, DC, having also spent a summer in Mississippi in 1965, which followed the Mississippi summer in which these young people were killed. So I was very interested in connecting ethics and Christianity to that kind of tumultuous concern for racial justice and the kind of violence that was going on in American cities, first of all in the South, then in other American cities where people were resisting the kind of changes that were needed in terms of historical racism in American society.

ॐ ॐ ॐ

Soul Searching *also provided me the privilege of meeting Daniel Berrigan, the esteemed Jesuit priest, activist, and poet. I interviewed him on a snowy December day at Corpus Christi Church in New York City, the site of Merton's baptism. Because of the inclement weather and a pending transit strike, I worried that Fr. Berrigan, then in his*

mid-eighties, might not be able to make it to the interview. At the sched-
uled hour he appeared, alone, precisely on time, brushing snow off his
jacket accumulated during the fifteen-block walk from his home. My
most vivid impression of the conversation was his obvious affection for
his old friend Tom Merton. I suspect that's why he came out on such a
snowy day.

❧   ❧   ❧

Daniel Berrigan: Well, I was teaching in Jersey, I was not yet ordained, and *The Seven Storey Mountain* came out and I read that with great interest and wrote Merton at that point. That would be about '48, I think. He was not allowed to enter into real correspondence at that point, so he just sent a signed card or something with a word of thanks on it. We really got started with the friendship around, oh, let's say, '60. I think I was teaching in Syracuse, and he had written an article for *The Catholic Worker* on the danger of nuclear war. I was very taken by it. I was very, very disturbed actually, and wrote him and said, "Thank you. I wish we were all taking this whole question more seriously." He wrote back and said, "Well, why not come on down and let's talk." So I did, and the abbot [James Fox] was very kind about the whole thing. He said if I would give a talk to the community he would pay my airfare, and that perdured virtually every year until Merton's death. I was down there every year.

Well, of course Merton's reputation was already very large by then, and several of his works were attaining a stature of classics, especially the autobiography. I didn't know what to expect when we first met. I was quite young at the time and had never dealt with anyone who was so much in the public eye, in such an ironic way because he was a contemplative and yet he was a celebrity. But what happened when I got there was very simple and very nice. It amounted to meeting someone

Merton's desk.

who was totally kind of unselfconscious about anything like fame, who was very much himself—plainspoken, warmhearted, open to friendship, and very modest about his attainment. So I went home the first time saying to myself, "Why, the chemistry was very good, and I think we're going to be good friends." And it happened that way.

What I chiefly remember about correspondence with Merton was the fact that we were each a very great help to one another in a couple of crises in our lives. Mine having to do with the civil rights movement and the freedom rides, and his having to do with censorship in the Order of some of the books he desperately wanted published that were not published. So I think we threw one another a lifeline at those points and he warning me, or underscoring the fact, that this was one crisis and there were going to be others and that it was a bad time to make any kind of crucial decisions about one's own future. I needed reminding at that point, because I was desperately disappointed and unhappy with the decision that I couldn't go on a freedom ride. And then I had to assure him that he had a few years ahead of him too, a few more crises, so he should take it slow, which he did.

Interreligious Dialogue

At virtually every showing of Soul Searching *I get a question that begins with, "What would Merton have thought. . . ." It's very flattering that someone would think I might have a clue about Merton's inner workings. Obviously I don't have any more than a clue, so I always couch responses with "my best guess" or something to that effect.*

My best guess is that Merton would have loved the Festival of Faiths that is held annually in Louisville and been proud of the host community he sometimes disparaged in his journals. Every year in the fall Louisville welcomes spiritual leaders for a remarkable weeklong festival of sharing religious traditions and embracing our common spiritual path. The Festival embodies the interfaith dialogue and exploration that

Merton became known for in the 1950s and 1960s. At the 2006 confer-
ence I had the honor of talking with Dr. Martin Marty, one of the most
respected observers of religion in America for more than fifty years. I
could think of no better person to consider Merton's contributions to
ecumenism and interfaith dialogue.

Martin Marty: Two movements grew up roughly during the time of
Merton's prime. One was Christian ecumenism, which had existed in
the modern form since 1911 in Orthodoxy and Protestantism, but
Roman Catholicism was not to take part until a new phase developed
with the Second Vatican Council (1962–65). The second was the interfaith movement that included Protestants, Catholics, and Jews that developed through World War II and after. I don't think many people were
thinking a good deal about what either of these movements meant for
religions of the East, which so fascinated Merton. I think he found that
if you went deep enough in Christian devotion, you could meet on
many things that the Hindus and Buddhists were about, and, if you
read them well, you would see that these could be congruent. I don't
think many people were talking about it at that time. A couple of
scholars were doing it, but Merton modeled those I prefer to think of as
agents, people who were active in interfaith dialogue with religionists of
the East.

Now, I don't think he'll be remembered as much for pioneering
work on ecumenism, simply because he had a lot of company there, but
he will be remembered as a pioneer on interfaith relations. His address
to monks of the East and West at Bangkok, Thailand, right before he
died by electrical shock in an accident, crystallized his being a pioneer
on interfaith relations. His death in Asia has become a kind of parable
or paradigmatic thing: "Oh, Thomas Merton, that's what he was doing
on the day of his death; maybe his life led up to that."

Bonnie Thurston: I think that Merton would have stopped exploring other traditions if he had felt he was compromising his basic life direction. He was a person of extraordinary openness in a decade of extraordinary openness. I mean these are the 1960s we're talking about and people were open on all kinds of levels. In a sense Merton's openness to other religions was part of the *zeitgeist*. People were very open to experimentation at the time. Eastern traditions had come into the popular consciousness in America by the 1960s. No, I don't think he was compromising his Catholicism at all. I understand that the church was a little uneasy about it, that the hierarchy was uneasy about Merton's interest in Buddhism and other religious traditions, but I don't think he was. I think in fact he felt it a call to do so. There's a passage in *Conjectures of a Guilty Bystander* when he actually says that it's incumbent upon some Christians to be open to other religious traditions and to engage them deeply. That it's really part of one's faithfulness to Christ to be open to the other. And that's theologically good thinking, because if it's true, as we Christians claim it is, that we have a universal Christ, a Christ who is open to all the people in the universe, not just on our planet, but the whole of the created universe, then why would it be wrong to be open to other people, other ways, other traditions?

I think that there is continuing dis-ease about Merton's interest in other religious traditions. I try to take a broad historical view of things and it seems to me that the pendulum does indeed swing back and forth. The period of the 1960s and 1970s was a period of really great openness after the Second Vatican Council, and the pendulum swung quite far in one direction. Now it's swinging quite far in the other direction, in a more conservative, and perhaps closed, perhaps not, way.

I think the degree of Merton's "openness to the other" does alarm some people. There are persons who think, and I happen not to be one of them, but there are persons who believe that Merton's openness to other religious traditions was in some way a betrayal of Christ and would fly in the face of things that Jesus says, like "No one comes to the Father but by me." I don't think Merton felt that at all. His openness was an openness to the universal Christ. The current spiritual scene is very different from what it was in the 1960s. It's more polarized now. People who want to be more exploring in the spiritual realm often leave the church, for example. They don't try to maintain dual citizenship, if I can put it that way. What I think Merton did, that I find so interesting, is that he remained firmly in the church and made these journeys out to other traditions. You can't be a pilgrim unless you have a home to go back to. You can't really travel safely in other waters unless you know where the harbor is. My way of reading Merton is that he was very clear about home and harbor, and that gave him immense freedom to explore in other traditions, in other places. I don't think he could have gone nearly as deeply in Buddhism and Islam had he not been so sure of his own identity, his identity as a Christian monk.

I think Merton was sort of spiritually ADD [attention deficit disorder] in a way. He was obviously a person of immense energy. I'm really searching for the right adjective. "Restless" is not the adjective I would use. He had an omnivorous intellect, that's how I would say it, he had an absolutely omnivorous intellect. He was interested in practically everything. That was true not only in the spiritual realm, but it was true in literature, it was true in music, it was true of people, it was true of politics. If you look at the people with whom he corresponded it's just an astonishing array of people. So I would say it's not that he was restless and dissatisfied with Christianity in some way, but that he had this omnivorous intellect about all kinds of things, and his spiritual curiosity was one manifestation of something that characterized him in general. So I think I would see it a little more neutrally than the way some people do.

There's plenty of correspondence in which Merton disagreed with his superiors and tried to reorganize his monastic life in various ways. He wasn't hidden about that. There's absolutely no indication that he ever wanted to be released from his monastic vows. It was no movement toward exclaustration, the technical term for leaving a monastic community. There was no sense that he did not want to fulfill his responsibilities as a priest in the church. He offered Mass regularly and was happy to do so. I just don't see any indication that something was lacking for him in Christianity. It's just that it's a big world, and it's a big world seen and unseen. We confess in the Creed that God created all things seen and unseen, and if we take that seriously, I think we're invited as Christians to explore in the unseen realm. Merton took that more seriously than most of us do.

I think Merton was one of the groundbreaking persons, one of the pioneers. I would want to make a distinction between ecumenism and interreligious dialogue. Ecumenism means "within the household." So ecumenism is properly a term that means Christians talking to Christians. Baptists to Catholics, Catholics to Lutherans, etc. Interreligious or interfaith dialogue is really the more accurate term for Merton and Judaism, or Merton and Islam, or Merton and Buddhism. I do think he was one of the pioneers of this kind of interreligious dialogue. He was one of the first people to formulate the principles for such dialogue. He was one of the first people to engage personally with persons of other faiths. That's where Merton was a genius. He was apparently such a warm and inviting person that he met persons of other religions easily and invited them to speak on a really deep level and was able to establish connection with them in ways that then led to real important dialogue, not only with Buddhism but with the Jewish tradition and Islam as well.

He knew more about some fields than he did about others. There's no question about it. There were fields in which he had read deeply and really was authoritative and there are other fields in which he was pretty superficial. I think that's fair to say, but there are an astonishing number of fields in which he really was very profoundly aware. I would say in both Buddhism and in the Sufi traditions of Islam Merton was very widely read, and had read the best scholarship that was available to him in the late 1950s and 1960s. Now, since then, we've had better sources translated into English, or better primary sources available to us, but in those two fields Merton had read the best that was available at the time.

Christine Bochen: The Dalai Lama said that Merton taught him what it meant to be a Christian, that in meeting Merton he had really met someone who was a Christian. And the exchanges that they had were exchanges and conversations that rested on their mutual respect for the other's practice and for the other's belief. Not minimizing those differences but being able to reach beyond them to a deeper unity that Merton not only knew about but can point the rest of us toward.

Robert Inchausti: Merton's view of interfaith dialogue was unlike a pluralism or relativism in which everybody's point of view is the same. He thought it was very important to engage other religious thinkers on their deepest conceptions of reality. And to try to agree with them and try to say yes as far as he could say yes, but if he didn't agree, to try to take all the things they affirmed, say yes to that, and yet go deeper as a way of affirming his commitments. Now if he could go deeper in a way that helped them go deeper, that is interfaith dialogue, because now you have two people authentically trying to make their lives deeper and more real. You don't have people trying to sort out dogmas and ideological concepts to make them fit schematically, which is a nice scholastic exercise, but that isn't faith that people live by. It isn't really honest. It's more like politics. It's more like, you know, religious diplomacy, which wasn't for Merton what religion was. For him it was a way of striking at a reality deeper than the contemporary world.

Merton found Eric Fromm's books very interesting, his book on the prophets, his book on love. He had a correspondence with Eric Fromm about the nature of modern society and its forces for alienation. He found all of those things very pertinent to his own spiritual quest. Merton wrote a very interesting essay, "Apologies to an Unbeliever." In it Merton says, "You know, atheists are given a bad rap by religious people because it takes a lot of faith and courage to be an atheist. You have to have a commitment to a certain set of values and ideals. Rather than just writing them out of the dialogue, writing them out of the conversation, they should be brought into the conversation of our search for deep-seated reality." So Merton was open to atheists. He was open to Marxists. He was open to anybody who was making an honest search for reality. He engaged in real dialogue in the sense of both persons trying to make the other person's position better, rather than two people trying to score points off one another or showing the superiority of their point of view. That's not dialogue. That's not even democratic discussion. That is sort of the pseudo-dialogue that has replaced real democratic discussion.

A lot of Merton's dialogues took place privately through letters and conferences, because the public domain is not often particularly generous to people who want to give a hearing to the alternative point of view. The culture critics that get the most play are the ones that are the most rigid and hold to extreme points of view and make their opponents look silly, which is the exact opposite of what Merton was all about. Merton's position was more like, "I don't really understand the beauty of atheism that a person like you would find it so compelling. Explain it to me. Show me what it is. And then, what is the God you don't believe in? I probably don't believe in that God either. And let's talk about what it is that we have in common, that allows us to say yes to one another." So interfaith dialogue, intercultural dialogue, became for Merton a very serious thing.

Citizen Merton

Everything I've read makes me think that Merton took vows very seriously, so it follows that American citizenship for him was more than an excuse to have a beer on the 4th of July. He had expectations of his adopted home and of his responsibilities as a citizen. As the Cold War and the nuclear arms race intensified in the 1950s, Merton responded by addressing the issues head-on in his writing. This opened him to criticism from many quarters, including the head of his own Cistercian Order.

෬ ෬ ෬

Lawrence Cunningham: I think that what happened in the late 1950s was that Merton, who had many interests, became interested in the peace movement. You have to remember this was during the height of the Cold War, and therefore to take a strong position against thermonuclear testing, or to take a strong position on banning the bomb, or to take a strong position on civil rights, especially after 1959, was to classify yourself as a "peacenik" or perhaps a communist. That charge was made against many people who were in this movement.

This was a time when the American bishops were strongly anticommunist, strongly in favor of the armament of the United States of America. They were fearful of the Russians, etc. Here we have this monk down in Gethsemani, in rural Kentucky, writing against war and signing peace petitions. So he becomes identified as a radical. In 1962 he was forbidden by the abbot general of the Order to write on certain issues involved with peace. He was silenced. Now the abbot general, Gabriel Sortais, was a former military chaplain, a Frenchman who was in favor of France having their own independent nuclear weapons. He was a great admirer of de Gaulle and here he had this crazy American monk talking about pacifism and so on. When John XXIII becomes pope and writes *Pacem in Terris*, Merton writes a letter and says, "Now that the pope is writing about peace, maybe I will begin to be able to write about peace."

When Merton was forbidden to write on these subjects, he obeyed and never published another word over this period. He does, however, write letters which he mimeographs and just sends them to friends. He calls these *The Cold War Letters*. Merton had a genius for puns. His title referred to the cold war between himself and the abbot general as well as to the so-called Cold War between the Soviets and the Americans. The strategy that Merton was using was the strategy that every dissident in Eastern Europe was using against the Marxist governments of their era.

Paul Elie: Merton played a number of roles in the emerging Catholic peace movement in the 1960s. He was a kind of father figure/elder brother to many of the Catholics for peace. He was a little older than they were. He had been famous for a number of years and he had been nonviolent since the 1930s. They looked to him as a wise man, as a guide, as someone who would show them the way forward. At the same time he was much more a moderate than a number of people in the movement. On the one hand he was more moderate than, say, Dorothy Day. Dorothy Day was a pacifist. She thought "all violence is wrong." Merton was nonviolent. It's a subtle distinction but an important one. He thought there were instances in which it was appropriate to commit an act of violence: direct self-defense of oneself and one's family. If a marauder is coming at you literally with a knife or a gun, it's permissible to protect yourself bodily and to protect your family. A true pacifist would say, "No, reason with that person. Pray with them but don't commit any violence yourself." So in that respect Merton was more moderate than many of the absolute pacifists.

On the other hand, he was more moderate than people who thought that violence against property, for example, was appropriate in the name of the message of peace. These people in the Catholic peace movement made a distinction between violence against property, particularly property owned by the government, and violence against persons. They would say, "What is the destruction of a few pieces of paper, draft cards or draft files, compared to the American forces' destruction of entire villages with napalm every day in Vietnam. There is no comparison." But Merton was very reluctant to authorize any destruction of property in the name of peace. So in this sense he was a man in the middle who was able to offer some balance and moderation to people on the front lines from his hermitage at Gethsemani.

Richard Sisto and Thomas Merton. Sisto today is an accomplished jazz musician and meditation teacher. He composed the music for Soul Searching *and shared many invaluable insights.*

In some respects Merton's views on the issues of the day didn't really change after he became a Catholic. He was always nonviolent and against war. He was always for racial tolerance and fairness. He was always against the commercial society and its distractions and its worship of the dollar. As the 1950s went on, these issues in their different ways became more pointed through American wars, through the gathering civil rights movement, through the beginnings of change in the church. Merton, again without really changing his views, became more outspoken, and this made people in the Trappist Order and in the church nervous. There was a concern that this literary Trappist was a little reckless and might be misleading some poor souls.

Lawrence Cunningham: Let's remember what's happening between 1965 and 1968. I remember these years quite well. We were having a collective nervous breakdown in this country. The cities were going up in flames in this country over civil rights. The antiwar movement was getting really ugly. They couldn't even hold the Democratic convention in Chicago in 1968 without riots. Martin Luther King Jr. was assassinated. Bobby Kennedy was assassinated. The Black Panther movement was moving. The peace movement was fragmenting, etc. It was a kind of a crazy time. And if you weren't somehow affected by the craziness, you had to be deaf, dumb, and blind.

Daniel Berrigan: I think there was a common understanding between Merton and me about the great social questions of the time such as the war or the civil rights movement. We felt ourselves in the same boat, and it was leaking, and we were rowing, and we were trying to throw water out. Keeping some sort of sense in our lives and some sort of continuity in our conscience, and I think those were parallel motions of the spirit.

I would say, especially with regard to the peace movement, we were very alone, and that the church was largely unawakened. Right through the course of the war, the bishops had nothing to say with regard to the crimes in Vietnam. In fact I was living here in New York City and Cardinal Spellman was actively promoting the war as a kind of a crusade against godless communism. It was all ideologically insane, and I was very unwelcome in all sorts of Catholic circles. I had come back from Europe—I was living in Europe in 1964–1965—and I remember saying to my brother Philip, "We better get started on the war or we never will," and he agreed with me. So we started the Catholic Peace Fellowship here in New York City and we got friendly with counselors, draft counselors, started all that work, and started really a kind of offensive presence around the cardinal, which he did not take lightly or well.

I never think of Merton as anything like a radicalizing influence on me, or myself on him, at least for awhile. My chief influence was my brother, and we were both in good places doing what I thought was worthwhile work. We were right in the middle of everything. We went to Selma together and met Dr. King for the first time and all these events had great impact upon me and I presume upon Merton secondhand.

The organizing of a retreat for peacemakers at Gethsemani was done by Merton and myself beginning about a year before, maybe 1964. This idea came to both of us while we were having a visit down there. Why not summon some people, ecumenical types across the spectrum, to come and do a few days of prayer together and talk about— what did Merton call it?—"The Roots of Dissent," I think that was his title. So we divided it up and each person consented to make a presentation, according to one's own background or tradition. People came from all over the place, Protestant and Catholic. I was trying to think if there were any Jewish members, but I don't think so. Then my brother Philip came barging in all the way from New Orleans with another priest. It was a very funny arrival, because the abbot had given orders to Merton that no Protestant present was to be invited to Communion, and Merton felt so badly about all of that, but he had to tell people, "I'm sorry but this is the order of the abbot." Well that didn't help matters at all, but Philip arrived in the middle of the Eucharist. He hadn't heard the order at all. So when Communion time came, Philip took it upon himself just to pass it to everybody. Thus it was solved. That was the nicest way, to come in late.

The friendship between the two men experienced some tension due in part to where each was coming from, Merton mindfully removed from the front lines and Berrigan breaching the barricades. I asked Fr. Berrigan his sense of this tension.

Daniel Berrigan: Well, we had a huge fracas break out at one point here in New York City because of the self-immolation of a young man in the Catholic Worker, Roger La Porte. He burned himself to death in front of the UN. And that was a huge crisis for all sorts of people in the city here. The cardinal was very preemptory in branding all this a suicide, which of course I had no sympathy with at all. I hadn't known this young man well, but I knew that he was not suicidal. I looked upon it much more as an act of self-immolation and sacrifice in favor of peace and against the slaughter. One had best be silent before an awesome occasion like this rather than putting a label on it and putting the young victim down. Anyway the reverberations of all that got to Merton, as they naturally would, and he being isolated, not knowing the circumstances, not being directly involved with any of these people or the community of the Catholic Worker, Merton fired off a telegram resigning from the Catholic Peace Fellowship, with a very strong implication that "if this is what is coming of my membership and all that, I want no more part in it." Well, that was a letter, I would say, of ignorance and of isolation and of no direct contact with circumstances of what was going on and the fever against the war here. So I gave it some time and then got down there and gave him some of the sense of the young man and sense of the way we felt about it. We had a Eucharist in his memory, I remember, right afterwards, and I spoke about it, I spoke of his death in terms of a gift, of a gift of himself rather than a fruit of despair, and that helped. So Merton cooled down.

142

I wondered if Berrigan was ever frustrated with Merton's stance.

Daniel Berrigan: Well, frustration was kind of a common mood of life itself because of the war. I think by and large, you know, that Merton made good decisions arrived at through prayer, and he talked to other monks about these matters, and he could easily have been sort of pulled into this vortex himself, because he was filled with such vitality and such passion. I wouldn't allow myself to sort of rest in the mood of alienation from him because he was making these choices. I didn't always understand, but I felt I had to trust him. In retrospect, I think, that was the better thing. You know, he was doing his service from there, and that was all right, you know.

The role of Merton was absolutely crucial. Philip would agree, I think, entirely, so would Jim Forest and Tom Cornell and the others. Correspondence with Merton and visits to Merton, prayer with Merton, the wisdom of Merton. He had a great gift for digging out the essentials of a situation like ours. He wrote, of course, one famous letter, I think it was to James Forest about the effect of something like this: "You will not survive America unless you undertake a discipline of prayer and sacrament. Period." That was the gist of that famous letter to a young peacemaker. I came deeply to believe that and to say that and quote that because I believed it so deeply myself. We saw so many young people give up, give in, walk away. It was a long hard road and we needed help along the way and he gave it. He gave it. He was very important to all of us.

Thomas had this image of a monk as being someone on the margins, at the edge, he would say. And he felt that that was a great advantage, because he could speak to people who were coming in and people who were leaving, and he could be there interpreting all sorts of lives of people who were not very clear about themselves. Well, I came to think that that was not the image I had about, let's say, my place in the scheme of things. I thought maybe his work, and mine as well, was not to look upon ourselves as at the edge of anything. We were creating a new center. We were where the Gospel required us to be, and the people who were giving in to violence as a Christian assumption, they were the people at the edge, not me. It was very clear to me and to Merton and to my friends that Christ was calling us to love our enemies and to do good to those who did ill to us. Peter put up your sword. Blessed are the peacemakers, not the war makers.

Father John Dear is happy to say he walks in the footsteps of fellow Jesuit Daniel Berrigan. Dear is also creating new paths suited to a different era of activism. I became aware of him initially through the book he wrote about living in Merton's hermitage after being in the penitentiary for civil disobedience. I arranged to come interview him near his home in New Mexico. In addition to the Santa Fe interview, I went with him and other protestors to the town of Los Alamos, the home of the atomic bomb. They were commemorating the sixtieth anniversary of dropping a nuclear bomb on Hiroshima, Japan.

Visiting a museum in Los Alamos, I saw one half of the stark divide in the American perception of nuclear arms. The theme of the museum was one of pride in accomplishment. It shows the town of Los Alamos growing in prosperity with the addition of new buildings and installations for bomb manufacturing. There are pictures of smiling new citizens of Los Alamos, prominent scientists who had come to help develop and manufacture the bomb. I couldn't help but think of Merton's poem, "Chant to Be Used in Processions Around a Site with Furnaces," which considers complicity with horrific acts done in the name of duty. As an American citizen reaping the material benefits of American power, I put aside the smug righteousness with which I was getting comfortable.

Outside the museum Fr. Dear and his colleagues were donning symbolic
sackcloth and smearing ashes on themselves. At the same time of day
the bomb was dropped on Hiroshima they sat silently and solemnly on
the sidewalks of Los Alamos for thirty minutes. The local police
watched warily. It seemed a familiar play in which the participants
knew their roles and the boundaries. On this day no one was arrested.
The last time I spoke with Fr. Dear he was contesting a judge's recent
ruling that would send him to prison for contempt of court relating to
another act of civil disobedience.

ॐ   ॐ   ॐ

John Dear: Thomas Merton's influence is still widely felt in the peace
movement—in all the movements for justice—here in the church in the
United States. During his lifetime, my friends, who were his friends in
the peace movement, called him the pastor of the peace movement. He's
certainly a great teacher of peace. He was breaking all new ground. He
was a teacher of peace for Daniel Berrigan, and even for Dorothy Day
of the Catholic Worker movement, and for a lot of grassroots peace activists young and old. Because here was this wise monk and a prominent writer speaking very clearly about nuclear weapons, the Vietnam
War, racism, and the civil rights movement and where it was going, but
then going deeper and talking about what are we supposed to be about,
and unpacking what he called the theological and spiritual roots of
Christian nonviolence. I think he wrote some of the most powerful essays on Christian nonviolence that went beyond what Martin Luther
King Jr. had time to write about or even what Mahatma Gandhi could
write. His writing on Christian nonviolence still stands today.

So, he helped found the Catholic Peace Fellowship, which became
the precursor to Pax Christi in the United States, which is part of the
international peace movement. What we have today, which is widely accepted around the world, is a mainstream Catholic movement for peace
and disarmament and justice that Merton helped sow the seeds for. He

never had the support that we have now. In fact, I've learned recently how Pope John XXIII read Merton and was particularly influenced by some letters from Merton, and that may have led him to write *Pacem in Terris* just before his death. And some of the monks at Gethsemani told me that when they met Pope Paul VI he said to them, "You were with Thomas Merton," and he was very excited. After the death of Pope John Paul II, I read that in his bedroom, in his personal library, he had all the collected works of Thomas Merton and had been reading them all his life.

I submit that we'll never really know the deep influence of Merton on all of us. Today in the Catholic peace movement in the United States, anyone who is serious about working to stop war and nuclear weapons and the direction the country is going in has learned the lesson of Thomas Merton: that this work is so hard, and that we're in for such a long haul, that it's got to begin with contemplative prayer. Merton taught us all that, and we're learning that lesson. And that's different from where the peace movement was in the 1960s. I hope we've matured or we're deepening, so that we're not just angry activists. We are spiritual people who are trying to move toward the God of peace as Merton called us to, as Merton did. Therefore not just denouncing war but inviting us to a vision of peace for the whole human race, and that's a great, great gift. So as I travel the country and talk to Catholic peace activists and activists of all the different religions, Merton's name comes up still. I wonder sometimes if Merton is more influential now than even in his own lifetime. He's bigger than he ever was, and he's going to continue to blossom and bear good fruit.

That's a great, great mysterious lesson for all of us, even if we think, as Merton said, our lives are ineffective because we're working to end war and we're making no difference whatsoever. Merton wrote to some of the peace activists and said, "Don't be distracted by that, we're on to something much deeper, the apostolic war toward the truth, toward our common humanity, and toward the God of peace. If you really go deep into that in the spiritual life, then we're into something much bigger than anybody really understands, and our lives will bear great fruit, because God is using them in ways we could never see." Merton's life shows us that now. The rest of us, I think, are trying to catch up to him. Do the good because it's good, as he would say. Pursue the truth because it's truthful, regardless of the outcome or how effective we may appear to be in the short run. We're keeping our eyes on the long haul, like Merton, and trusting the God of peace to use us in ways that we can't imagine for some great day down the road when disarmament will actually happen.

I think Thomas Merton was a really radical Christian in the real meaning of the word "radical," which comes from the Latin meaning "root." He went to the root of Christianity. That's why he's not a liberal or leftist; he's actually a real conservative in the sense that he's going all the way back to the saints and the prophets, into the Bible, into the early church and into the life of Christ himself. So that Merton didn't want to be just a great writer or even a great activist. He wanted to be a saint, and he became a holy prophet. Now that is something, you know, that God did, which makes him more radical than anybody. I mean he's up there with Martin Luther King Jr. and Dorothy Day, who may be canonized, and Daniel and Philip Berrigan, as an instrument of the God of peace to the world. People can dismiss him, "Well he was against war, nuclear weapons, and, you know, our country is a great country and we're patriotic people." But if you're serious about your Christianity or your Catholicism or just the spiritual life, and you're going deep, deep, deep, like Thomas Merton, who for twenty-seven years spent seven hours in prayer a day, you're going to end up going deep into the life of Christ, to the meaning of the Gospel, and seeking the truth and plumbing the contemplative depths of universal love. So you end up very peacefully and calmly saying things like, "These weapons are immoral, the Vietnam War is unjust, no white Christian can practice racism,"—and, I think, he would now add sexism—"and we all have to go deep into the roots of nonviolence."

People say, "Well, Merton, maybe he was just a dangerous loose cannon." Actually I think he was at the heart of the church, because he was at the heart of Christ, bearing witness in a new, creative way to our culture, about what the Gospel means, and what it means to follow Jesus, and what it means to be a peacemaker, a son or daughter of the God of peace. What does it mean to explore the spiritual life? It means to go really deep into love, and really deep into living in peace with the whole human race. It means seeing every human being on the planet as your sister and brother. In other words, it means really beginning to see the world from the perspective of God. I think Merton, in the best Trappist sense, put on the mind of Christ, as St. Paul said, and when you do that you're just living in a different realm. Really you're going deep into that great nonviolent love for all people. He's gone ahead of us and called us all to try and really go deep into the root of the Gospel and into the meaning of the life of Christ here and now.

We still, in our clericalism, seem to think, "Well, it was easy for Merton because he was a hermit. He had time to work this through." No, I think he actually agonized more about Vietnam, or where we were going with nuclear weapons, than anybody. His life was really a life of pain and sorrow. And like the true prophets, if you read Isaiah and Ezekiel and Jeremiah, his life was a life of grief and mourning and begging God for mercy upon the whole human race. That's why he identified with Jonah in *The Sign of Jonas* and being a prophet in the belly of the beast. That's a very painful life.

And Merton gives us courage, I think, through his intellect and wisdom to say, "This is what it means to be a Christian. Go ahead and do it and suffer through it and trust that your life is going to bear good fruit." That's why we all, especially in these times, with the wars going on in the world and the thousands of nuclear weapons that continue to exist and the poverty and racism and sexism, need to go deep into the spiritual life and figure this out for ourselves and begin to stand up, and publicly bear witness.

In many ways I think Merton had it harder. We all can have communities and form local communities to support each other and talk these things through and help each other become nonviolent and then go to protests and write our Congress people and speak out in our church. We've come a long way and gotten a lot more support than Merton ever had alone in his hermitage. So I always think that if Merton could do it, we've got to do it.

Kathleen Deignan: Thomas Merton always understood himself in some sense to be a prophet in the belly of a paradox. He always, like a good prophet, has had an unsettling effect on all who engage his wisdom and teaching. That was true in his life and I suppose in some ways continues to be true even now. I would say especially now that we have had the opportunity to explore more of his legacy as his journal writings have come to be available to us. Merton's fierce social consciousness and conscience will not let us move from the Jesus tradition of nonviolence. This is very, very disquieting. Merton disturbs us and has been disturbing us since he began writing in a number of arenas. One arena is in his social criticism, his unrelenting commitment to the nonviolence of Jesus. It's very, very difficult for the Christian tradition to really honor the extreme nonviolence of Jesus and find its home in the world at the same time. I think, within the Christian tradition, we have made our agreements or compromises with what we call reality. Merton didn't go there. Although I think he was a realist, he stayed very much on the side of this prophetic witness of Jesus and the early gospel tradition, to the way of nonviolence, to the celebration of life at all cost, within an empire of death. Merton remained incredibly faithful to that and, if we do a reading of his writings on nonviolence, on war, on poverty, on racism, on injustice, his writings are as relevant and contemporary today as when he was writing in the 1950s and 1960s. His writings have an uncanny relevance, a disquieting, uncomfortable relevance.

Paul Elie: I don't think Merton can be seen as part of the New Left for a variety of reasons. It's true that he was sympathetic to the New Left's critique of modern society. For example he liked Herbert Marcuse's *One-Dimensional Man* as an interesting analysis of how technological

society empties individual lives of depth and content. He liked Eric Fromm's *The Art of Loving*, which has a whole section about how bourgeois culture empties depth out of human experience and turns it into more of a commercial lifestyle. But as much as he liked their critique, he didn't find in them any answer and proscriptive side. He liked them in their descriptive side but didn't like them in their proscriptive side. He agreed with a lot of their critiques of contemporary consumer society, but he didn't think the answer lay in a Marxist totalitarian critique of history.

In fact, if anything, an answer demanded something that transcended a totalitarian, Marxist, Hegelian critique of history, which meant a sort of honest, Christian, interior exploration of conscience. So the way you defeat a runaway mass media is not to put mass media in the hands of certain correct thinking, totalizing ideologues who know the truth. The way you defeat it is by dismantling its false influences in your own life, seeing through its illusions, so you can get back at some reality. The way you do that is through internal development, through prayer, through retreat, through reflection, not through culture wars or ideological posturing. And that's a deeper, more essential thing that takes more time, that works through generations, that is part of what is best in culture, is truth seeking and honest, not ideological posturing and cheap victories. And so that's why he's not, I don't think, a man of the New Left.

Robert Inchausti: I guess a case could be made that Merton, in becoming a monk and backing off from some of his more radical statements about the Vietnam War, was not as aggressive a social critic as some of his more secular, radical peers. There is a kind of worldly courage, of throwing yourself into the battle. I think Rollo May, Norman Mailer, and Allen Ginsberg, writers of that period, had that physical courage of

Merton's second hermitage was located about a mile from the monastery on a hill he named Mount Olivet.

throwing themselves into a social fray without really knowing where they were going or where it was leading, but they were willing to take a chance and a shot at altering the cultural equation. I think Merton's courage was a different kind of courage. His courage was in saying, "That's good, but my vocation is to find reality, not necessarily change the political calculus of my time. And so that means that I have to stay true to the logic of my vocation and my calling, which means that I'll have my say, but I won't redefine myself by terms that are defined by the world."

So in retrospect Merton's statements on the war, Merton's statements on nonviolence, continue to have a relevance that some other statements, like those that came out of the "Human Being Rally" in San Francisco, or even some of the speeches that were made in Chicago in 1968, do not. They're gone. They don't have a contemporary relevance. They've been redefined by history, they've been sort of recontextualized and diminished. Merton's work can't be so easily dismissed because it was never so contemporarily conceived. I think he knew that. He knew who he was and what his calling was about, and so he knew that he had to give up on that front of contemporary relevance in order to gain on the long-term front of honest witness. Who knows what takes more bravery? In some ways it takes more physical bravery to deal with the stupidities of one's era while they're happening, but it isn't as wise maybe, or it isn't as honest as someone who backs away and says, "OK, I might make a show of myself right now, but in the long run the truth will win out, and I have to be on the side of truth."

There were people who wrote him letters and said, "Why don't you leave the monastery and join the movement?" He said, "Well, you know, this is who I am, this is my community, this is where I live, and I'm not a cerebral person that believes in history the way you believe in history, you know. I believe that I can comment on what's happening, but the only reason I can comment on it is because I live outside of it. And once I throw myself into it, then I'm going to be subject to the same sort of political turmoil that you are." So that's the choice he made. I think in the long run, looking back on his continuing influence, it was the right choice for him. I don't think it's necessarily the only choice, or the best choice for everybody. I think the Berrigans were more willing to enter into contemporary politics, and they respected Merton, and Merton respected them. Dorothy Day is another great example of somebody who entered into contemporary policy issues with her faith to a degree I don't think Merton ever really did. I think that has to do with his own sensibility, his own literary background, and his own sort of theological take on history.

Martin Marty: I never met Thomas Merton and we didn't really correspond. We had only a couple of contacts and the most vivid one was when he wrote his most severe and radical critique of society, in which he even envisioned possible concentration camps in which you put blacks because they were black, and things like that. Well, I reviewed it, I think for the old *New York Herald Tribune*, and I said, "This time I think you went too far. Things are bad, but I can't picture the government doing all this," and so on. It was the same week in which, I think in *Commonweal*, he reviewed one of my books very favorably. I went to my editor at *The Christian Century* and said, "What am I going to do?" He said, "Well, I would do this," and that was exactly how I approached him: "Dear Father Louis, I have read your review of my book and you've probably read my review of yours. We could both be wrong." And I think it was a nice neutralization.

Then a few years later, I think in the form of a column, I went back and apologized publicly to Merton when we realized that the administration had deceived. It had lied. It had stimulated revolutionary movements for which it needed counterrevolutionary movements, and many of the things that Merton had said came about. I tend to be, as a historian, a little more patient with history I suppose, and I see gains, incremental gains, when you have them. William James talked about "meliorism," doing what you can to make it somewhat better, but I think prophets like Thomas Merton, like Mother Mary Luke Tobin of the Loretto Sisters, and, in our more recent times, like Sister Joan

Chittister and so on, they could just look right through it all and just say, "We don't have to compromise that much. We don't have to muffle our voice that much." And I think what they do is project something that the rest of us can say, "Well, I'm not going to go that far, but you did hit my conscience," and I think Merton did that for many people.

Elena Mailits: One of the things I find most interesting in Thomas Merton is that he adamantly refused to let himself be called a conservative or a liberal. He did not like to be put into boxes with labels on them. He said that deprived him of his freedom to think on the other side. He was fiercely determined that he not be so identified with a particular group that it destroyed his capacity to enter into another point of view and see the value of that. So he would not let himself be called liberal or conservative or stop any place on the spectrum. He did things and said things that alienated people who did fall into those categories. Some of the things he wrote just infuriated the people who wanted him to stay with the beliefs and attitudes that he had expressed in *The Seven Storey Mountain.* They were furious at the things he wrote in a book like *Conjectures of a Guilty Bystander,* where he condemned the commercialism of American society and where he was so infuriated with the military industrial complex. When he wrote all of his antiwar things during the Vietnam War, a lot of people stopped reading Merton, but he opened up a whole new audience. These are people who to this day don't know what to make of *The Seven Storey Mountain* but are fascinated by a book like *Faith and Violence* or anything he wrote on the Taoists or in his Asian journals.

Learning to Love

The period of Merton's life during which he falls in love with his nurse presented me with some of the most delicate questions of the entire project. As a commercial producer I knew that the material was compelling. It had many elements of great drama, not the least of which was the combination of forbidden love and a spring–fall romantic pairing. This was also material that had not been public knowledge when Paul Wilkes made his documentary.

Reactions to my depiction of this period have been mixed. I'll quote the acclaimed Merton scholar Christine Bochen: "I think as people read the account of Merton's falling in love, they respond in ways that say much more about them than about Merton." This applies to readers, audience members, and filmmakers. I can say that at showings people are very attentive during this segment. There are few guaranteed laugh lines in a documentary about a monk, but I can almost always bank on chuckles when it is related how Merton and Dom James Fox dealt with each other on this issue. As with most work I can now see ways I would've done it differently, but my hope is that I accomplished my goal of showing Merton's humanity without being exploitive.

Christine Bochen: In 1966, while Merton was hospitalized, he met and fell in love with a nurse, a student nurse, a young woman who was assigned to his care. And for a short time, during the spring and summer of 1966, that relationship absorbed a great deal of his energy. It was certainly a most surprising thing for him, and it is surprising for many who read the story, but read in the context of Merton's life it was an experience, certainly not the only experience that we should pay attention to, but an important one.

Merton's experience of falling in love is an experience that we might look at through a number of lenses, and from a number of sides. As editor of the journals that relate his experience, in volume 6 of the journals entitled *Learning to Love*, I was very mindful of Merton's candidness and willingness to speak out about this aspect of his life's story, and I thought it admirable. But I worried, frankly, that in telling his own story he was also telling hers, and she had made no decision to tell the story. I think as people read the account of Merton's falling in love, they respond in ways that say much more about them than about Merton. I remember speaking about the journal shortly after it came out and hearing lots of different responses. I remember one nurse said to me, "Oh, it's perfectly understandable. When men of that age are in the hospital, they regress." Another, and it happened to be that this was another nurse, a woman of mature years, said, "You know, I think a great deal of this was in his head." And I thought, you know, in many of the ways in which persons respond, they say something about how it is that they look at life, how it is that they look at human personalities.

In the most recent class that I taught on Merton, my students were reading *The Intimate Merton*, the compilation of journals. There was an interesting exchange on the evening for which they read the selections from volume 6. On one side of the room was a group of students who said, "This is wonderful. Merton has discovered something he didn't know before." On the other side was a group of students very concerned, saying, "Oh, don't go there. Remember, he's a monk." This tension, I think, between a recognition that this was an experience that had deep significance in Merton's life, but was also an experience that was in some ways at odds with his commitment as a monk, creates a kind of struggle or paradox in our interpretation. Reading the journals, we recognize that Merton knew early on that this was a relationship that really could not continue, that in the course of it he reaffirmed his vows.

Merton recognized that he was a monk and he was a monk committed to this community and to this life, and he was very much aware of that from the beginning of that relationship. I think we need to be reminded that it was actually a relationship that was very short-lived. And that they actually met and were together very few times, talked on the telephone, had some exchange through correspondence. So it's easy, I think, to expand the relationship beyond the time that was actually involved, to look at that relationship now as somehow dominating Merton's consciousness even in those years, and it did not. It was a short, very intense period of time, a meaningful time.

What did this relationship mean for Merton? We really don't know. We can only speculate. Merton certainly recognized the significance of his commitment to monastic life, and reaffirmed that commitment, and knew that this love could not lead, would not lead, to another way of life. So he knew that the relationship had to end. What did he learn? We don't know that either. I've heard others reflect on the role of this experience in Merton's personal development, and I find myself holding back from an interpretation. It's too easy to tie up the messiness of one's life in a neat little package and say something like, "Well, Merton grew," or "Merton needed this experience in order to resolve his relationships with women." I'm not really given to that easy solution. A short time afterwards, in the following year, we find in Merton's journal that he burns the letters that he has received from her. He doesn't say much else there, and my question, my wondering is, what might he have said had he lived longer? How might he have seen that relationship and understood it had he lived another ten years? It seems to me that Merton took a long time to reflect on earlier relationships with women, and it's not until 1965 or so that we find him revisiting and characterizing earlier relationships. Perhaps it is only Merton himself who could have told us what the significance of that relationship was for him.

The experience of editing a journal is an experience that I share with other editors of Merton's complete journals, but the experience of editing volume 6 was in some ways a distinctive one because of the nature of a portion of that journal, and it is only a portion of that period through 1966 and through October of 1967. I can remember very well the day in which I received a copy of the journal pages, and I remember sitting with the package and thinking for a while about what an awesome responsibility this was. I remember thinking that I was looking at pages that very few people had seen. I presumed that the general editor, Brother Patrick Hart, had seen these pages. I presumed also that Michael Mott had seen them. But there I was, looking at a story, and I'm speaking here of the journal itself, of this period within Merton's life that included some very private and some very personal experiences,

and I was one of the very few people who had seen it. I was very mindful of the fact that I was entering into, especially in those pages, into an exchange of a story that involved two people. One of whom had given me permission to enter in to read the story. I kept being mindful all the way through that I was reading Merton's account of this experience and of this relationship, and I couldn't help wondering what the other side of the story might be like. I, as an editor of the journals, recopied this holographic journal written in Merton's hand into my own hand. I did not sit at a computer with this journal, and my friends who know my handwriting chuckled at that and said that was little progress. But I felt that experience allowed me to listen in on
Merton's own personal reflections as I read entry by entry. So it was exciting to be an editor of the journal and particularly, I think, of that journal. And I was also aware of the responsibility I had. I wanted in my introduction to present the story of that relationship in context. It would be unfortunate, I think, if Merton's relationship with her became the only lens through which we looked at the Merton of the late 1960s or the Merton living in the hermitage on the grounds of Gethsemani.

He was older, presumably should have been wiser, recognized early on that the relationship could not continue, so there's no way in which I want to create of this a neat package. I think the most that we have here is the story of a human being's struggle with all of the dimensions of human life, with sexuality, with love, with the need for human intimacy. I don't find myself needing, nor wanting, nor being able to impose a meaning on this experience; in fact I hold back from doing it.

Anthony Padovano: While I was in the midst of writing a book on Merton, *The Human Journey, Symbol of a Century*, I came across in my research, in the early 1970s, some indication that Merton had had a very substantial relationship with a nurse whose name was Margaret. As far as I could determine, that was nowhere in print. No one except an extremely small circle of people knew about that. When I came across it, I was in a struggle about what to do with it. I was jolted because it forced me to rethink many of my categories and to consider how I would eventually evaluate this man and his spiritual journey. I had to first of all verify that what I had discovered was true. The two people that I thought I would most want to hear from on this were his abbot James Fox, who demanded that the relationship end, and who went to Merton for confession, and Flavian Burns, to whom Merton went to for confession. So I asked both of them about this.

What surprised me was that both of them discounted it as a liability. I said to James Fox, "Maybe a lot of your negative readings on Merton you may feel are justified in light of this." And he said, "Absolutely not. It has nothing to do with who he was. I don't see that as negative. I would not go in that direction." I found this rather surprising. What I also thought was surprising was that Fox did not, as many American bishops might, throw a lot of holy water on it and get very pious about it and so on. He just said, "No, he fell in love. Those things happen. And then he continued with his monastic life." He didn't say this last thing in so many words, but he didn't see the relationship as a failure. Then, when I asked Flavian Burns about it, he said, "In no way does this detract from him as a mystic." So these were two people whose insights I would probably value as much as anyone's.

Paul Elie: Merton's involvement with the nurse in Louisville was a major episode in his life. It's impossible to pass over it now that we know about it. I understand it in the terms that he set forth in his other writings at the time, as an existentialist experience like those in Albert Camus. Here's a man who had written endlessly about love, the love of God, the love of other people, but who felt that his experience of love was limited. He was an orphan. He'd been raised in some instances by relative strangers. He had to ask himself, "Is my understanding of love real? Is what I have to say about love founded on anything?" At the same time he needed to test, existentially as it were, his vows as a Trappist monk. There was a lot of restlessness throughout the religious orders at that time and it's as if he was saying to himself, "Well, how real are my vows? How genuine is my calling to be a monk committed to celibacy, which is meant to keep me oriented toward God and God alone?" This sounds very cold and abstract, because he was very passionate about this nurse, but behind it all was his knowledge that he wanted to know what love is and what his understanding of it was. At the same time he wanted to know whether that part of his vows was genuine or just something not connected to his true being as a monk. Well, he decided that love was real but also that his calling was real, and his monastic calling ruled out carrying on with this nurse, so none too subtly he ended it.

James Conner: I learned of his relationship with Margie through something that he told me himself. And I can't say that I was either shocked or horrified or scandalized when I heard about it. It's never been that clear to me how far the relationship went. Whether anything really seriously, gravely sinful took place or not, only the Lord knows. But I felt very sorry for him at the time, because of the fact that he felt very crushed the way that the thing was revealed, that someone happened to listen in to a phone conversation that he was having with Margie. And it was one of the brothers who worked out at the switchboard and then told the abbot. The abbot of course confronted him about it, and he obviously felt very embarrassed by it. I know shortly after he'd spoken to me about it, it happened one day that I was up at the family guesthouse, and he came by there, and he had some lady with him. They had been out in the woods. She had come to visit him. As soon as Merton saw me I could tell that he was immediately very embarrassed. He even stopped me afterwards, later on, and, you know, made it clear to me that the lady was not Margie, that he was not continuing something in that way. So he obviously felt somewhat embarrassed by it. But personally I've never felt, you know, either horrified or scandalized at it. I have felt myself that in many respects it may have been one of the great graces of his life. Because he was someone who, due to the circumstances of his early life, always had something of a real question mark in his own mind about the whole issue as to whether he really was loveable himself, and whether he could really love, truly and honestly. And my impression is that the experience convinced him that he was truly loveable, could really be loved by someone to a very intense degree, and that he could love someone very intensely in return. So I felt that it was a real preparation for the end of his life in a sense, and maybe brought something of a greater wholeness to his own humanity, in a very painful way, certainly, but in a very real way, nonetheless.

Michael Mott: I think there are two really lasting things, one maybe positive and the other one possibly negative, that arose from his deep love of that particular summer, the summer of 1966. For the first time he was absolutely assured that he had been loved. That he was loveable. You can say the monastery is a school of love and all that sort of thing. This is different, very different. You go back and you think of the other women that had been in Merton's life at one time, altogether different. This wonderful woman shook him up and quite often said, "What are you talking about when you talk about solitude? You don't know about solitude? You don't know about this, that, and the other thing, and I'm about to show you about love." And she showed him, and he never doubted that he was loveable again, in that sense.

And the possibly slightly more negative result was it confirmed that he couldn't trust himself in this kind of situation, because he was out for two goals at the same time and the goals could not be reconciled. He was out for his solitude, the life he was leading at Gethsemani, and he was out for having a woman with him the entire time, and Gethsemani rules don't actually permit that. So he had to choose—either/or, buddy. And that really hurt, and it really hurt because it was so important. There's one poem of his where he talks about pretty well coming apart, his bones coming apart, coming apart as a human being. And I think many of us have been there, and we recognize that this was a tremendous struggle. It may have started out as kidding around and sending Snoopy cards to one another and all the rest of it, but it sure ended up in something that was serious and in some ways hurtful and in some ways magnificent. I try to deal with that in my biography, *The Seven Mountains of Thomas Merton*, and also to be fair to her. I think that she contributed a remarkable amount to Merton, and I know she, too, was suffering. All the evidence is that she suffered horribly from it.

William Shannon: Well, I think that whole episode is a very strange one in Merton's life. In some ways it was a good experience in a sense that he learned that he could love and be loved. I think he hadn't experienced that sort of thing in his life before. But I think he knew that eventually he would have to make a choice between her and his hermitage, and he knew what he would choose. So I'm not sure how fair he was to her when this whole relationship was going on. I'm not sure how much, and I must say that I hover back and forth between saying that it was really a deep love that he experienced, and it was a wonderful thing for him to experience that love, between that and a feeling that he was using her and that it was a fairly passing thing in his life. Because I think it was. It took place in 1966 and in the last journals he wrote, "I burned the letters from her the other day. I never even looked at one of them." In another place in the journals he writes about "the incredible stupidity of 1966," which seems to suggest that finally he thought of his experience as an expression of immaturity on his part, an expression of maybe a need that he had for some kind of sexual experience. I don't know. It's very hard, I find it very hard to evaluate that, to try to understand it.

John Eudes Bamberger: Well, I don't feel very free to go into that except to say that it was much more complicated than it sounds, the way I got involved. In any case, I did see Merton at that time. We discussed together his whole relationship with this woman and his whole way of handling it. I came away with a very positive impression of his position. He made no attempt at all to defend himself, made no excuses for himself. He sort of made fun of himself in a good way. And it took a lot of inner strength to do that. I was his student, you know, and yet he was very open and very defenseless at that time and was able to handle that and come away feeling that something worthwhile had happened through our exchange. I wouldn't say I counseled him, but I certainly dealt with the issue he was going through at that time. But he had already pretty well come to terms with the fact that the abbot already knew about it, and that was the end of the relationship in terms of personal contacts and so on. He accepted that, but he took all the blame on himself.

I think [the relationship] has been highly overplayed. If you read his journal entries after that, I think one of the most informative is the one where he says, 'this afternoon I burned all of her letters, and I felt nothing.'" It wasn't a wrenching experience, it was emotionally uninvolved. Although he himself, at the time he was involved with her, thought that it would change his whole life, I think there's evidence that it didn't have that much [impact]. The other statement that he makes in his diary is an indirect reference, or a masked reference, I should say, when he says, "Oh the summer of 1966, how foolish." That was his comment, "how stupid" or "how foolish." That's all he says, but that's what it meant to him when he got some perspective. So I don't think you speak that way if it really means as much as he thought it did when he was in it.

Jonathan Montaldo: The year before his death Merton sets up a legal instrument, the Merton Legacy Trust. His literary will stipulates that after twenty-five years following his death, part or all of his journals could be published. That tells me he wanted people to know about his relationship with the nurse. He wanted people to know about this young woman and his affection for her and what it meant to him. Merton always loved women. He loved them before he entered the monastery, and he loved them while he was in the monastery. He liked their company. I've met nuns who said they had danced with Merton on his hermitage porch. He was easy in their company.

There are indications, though, that Merton had problems of intimacy with women. In his journals, on the vigil of his fiftieth birthday,

January 30, 1965, he wrote, "One thing that I'm thinking about is sex, and how I never really handled that very well. All the women that I knew were conquests. I never had a real relationship with them." Somewhere else in his journals he wrote, "My chastity is maimed because I gave up something I never had. I gave up loving a woman by my vows and I never really loved a woman." So I think his encounter with the student nurse can be read one way as the opening of "the gate to the rose garden" that he had never entered.

He was a man who was fifty-one years old and was in a hermitage, solitary, sick. Many nurses tell me that their patients, their male patients, fall in love with them because they're cared for, talked to, in a moment of great vulnerability. You could look at it as a midlife crisis. But Merton felt that he learned something. He writes in his journals, "We have gone through something that both of us could never have learned any other way." And he felt that he was able to love this young woman and that she loved him for who he was in all of his craziness and weakness at that time. She must have been a very mature person to have dealt with so complicated an individual.

But Merton knew it had to end, and it does end, when one of his conversations with her on a Gethsemani telephone, which at that time had party lines, was overheard by a brother on phone duty who told Dom James what he had heard. Now Timothy Kelly, who was the abbot at Gethsemani for twenty-five years, told me recently a fact I did not know. Abbot Timothy told me that, when James Fox found out from this brother about this conversation, James Fox did not go directly to Merton. He told the cellarer, "Tell Father Louis that I know about this young woman." The cellarer goes to Merton and tells him, "The abbot knows." So James Fox didn't put Merton on the spot; he allowed Merton to come to him of his own accord. And Merton does go to the abbot and talks to him. And the relationship with Margie is virtually finished at that point. Not that Merton doesn't in his journals agonize about its finishing, but because he's able to go public with it with his abbot, he knows the relationship has got to tone down and end, and it does.

Daniel Berrigan: Oh yeah, it was a very dislocating time. I must say that I thought that the abbot handled that whole situation, which was very delicate and difficult, handled it well, and clearly, and drew some boundaries that needed to be drawn.

Paul Pearson: I'm of two minds of how significant Merton's relationship with the nurse in 1966 was. There's a part of me that feels that it was extremely important; I think Merton in his journals up until that period is concerned about his own ability to relate to women, his own ability to truly love. In some of his journals he reflected on the poor quality of some of his relationships with women prior to his entry into the monastery. And obviously his own lack of a mother figure, I think, must have played some part. And yet after his relationship with the nurse in 1966, he no longer talks about that difficulty, so I think it enabled him to make some kind of breakthrough. And certainly, one thing that surprised me was that the relationship with the nurse was in the early part of 1966, March and April, and by September 1966 Merton is taking a vow to remain in the hermit life, and I find that quite extraordinary. If he's really had such a rocky period, then, you know, I would have thought the abbot would have said, "Well, I don't think this is the right time to think about taking such a vow," but obviously the abbot thought that it was, and Merton thought it was. So in that sense, I think, there was some real deepening and moving forward in his life at that point so that he felt he was in a position to take that vow to live a solitary life for the rest of his life. And yet I think our understanding of that relationship with the nurse is one-sided. We only really know Merton's side of the story. You read that story in his journal from 1966 and you think, "Is this infatuation? What's going on here?" Without knowing her side of the story, it's hard to comment.

Asia

There was a time when I felt uneasy, maybe threatened, by reading of Merton's occasional restlessness in his life at Gethsemani. Sometimes you want an inspirational figure to stay as you originally found them, to be a constant polestar that's always in the same comforting place. The threat may have been that I realized that to continue in my appreciation of Merton I, too, would have to grow and stretch.

Reading of Merton's excitement in exploring other faith traditions, I came to appreciate how securely rooted he was in his embrace of God. He was so secure in it that he could examine other traditions, within Christianity and beyond, affirming the power and authenticity of these spiritual paths. It seemed that as at 4th and Walnut in Louisville, where he saw other people shining like the sun, he also saw illumination in other faith traditions. Despite the trepidation this created for some in the Roman Catholic hierarchy, I knew it was a key element of his journey that I wanted to share in Soul Searching.

John Eudes Bamberger: There was something restless in Merton, and that corresponds to being alive and to what life is. That's what made him a poet and a good writer and a good communicator. He was alive. And so, no one answer to life worked very long for Merton.

Bonnie Thurston: When one understands that Buddhism actually is an outgrowth of Indian thinking and philosophy, Merton's interest in Buddhism goes back to the time he was in school at Oakham in England, when he argued a pro-Gandhi position in a school debate—a debate, incidentally, that he lost. Then at Columbia he was reading Buddhist writings in French and wasn't very impressed. *The Seven Storey Mountain* doesn't give us a very positive view of Eastern religions in general. But during Merton's first ten years at Gethsemani someone had come to the community to do some painting work. The guy had been a Zen monk at one point and gave some talks to the monks about Zen. That really, according to Brother Patrick Hart, was Merton's first real personal contact with the Buddhist tradition.

Then from the 1950s on he was doing a lot of reading in Buddhism, particularly in the Zen tradition, because Zen was the tradition that had the most materials available in English at that point. At the end of his life he made his Asian pilgrimage and at that point became very interested in Tibetans and the Tibetan tradition. So he actually moved pretty much chronologically through Buddhism, from Indian thought to Theravadan thought and then into Zen and finally into the Tibetan tradition.

Buddhism certainly changed the way he wrote poetry. I wrote my doctoral dissertation on the effects of Merton's studies of Buddhism on his poetry. The poetry became much sparer, if I can use that as an adjective. The difference between a tree in full leaf and a tree without any leaves, where you see the structure of the branches, was really the change that happened in Merton's poetry, particularly, I think, as a result of his studies of Zen. The degree to which he actually practiced Zen is a little hard for us to know.

We have to be very cautious about reading journals, and the reason I say this is out of a profound understanding of my own ability toward self-deception. So when we read somebody's journals, we have to read them with a grain of salt: "Is this really the case or was this what he thought himself was the case?" You understand the issue? Merton changed so much in so many ways that I would be very hesitant to say, "Well, his change was because of the Buddhist tradition, per se." Because at the same time he was reading in the Buddhist tradition he was also reading in the Sufi tradition of Islam. He had correspondents all over the world, and certainly their ideas were profoundly affecting him. Whether or not the Buddhist studies encouraged his desire to be a hermit is hard to say, but I think it's likely. I don't think, say in his writing style or in the subject matter to which he attends in the journal, there's a lot of direct traceable influence to Buddhism.

There's certainly a fair amount in the journals in which he's reflecting on what he is reading. The other place to look at this, of course, is the working notebooks at the Thomas Merton Center at Bellarmine University; in those notebooks we really see what he was really thinking about when he studies Zen. It's a hard question, and it's a subtle question to ask how one's religious practice affects one's personality. It would be a hard question to ask anybody.

Brother David Steindl-Rast, a Benedictine monk who knew Merton, suggests that it was the Hindu monk Bramachari who precipitated Merton's conversion to Christianity by saying to Merton, when he was at Columbia, "What you really ought to do is to read Saint Augustine's *Confessions* and the great mystics of the Christian tradition," which Merton did, and then subsequently he became a Roman Catholic Christian.

Where one sees "the light going on" is in his long correspondence with D. T. Suzuki and in his book *Zen and the Birds of Appetite*, which is the result of their dialogue over a long period of time. I think what Zen provided for Merton, if I can shape the question this way, was threefold. It gave him a vocabulary to talk about experiences in the religious life that he had already had. So there was a point of convergence, and Zen gave to him a new vocabulary to talk about some of the inner experience that he had within the Christian tradition. Secondly, Zen was a cultural alternative for Merton. The Buddhist tradition for him was in part a metaphor for the alternative to the West, with its acquisitiveness, all of the things that have to do with Western culture in the 1960s. Zen was the alternative, Buddhism was the alternative, for Merton. And thirdly, because the Buddhist tradition has an ancient monastic strand, Merton found Buddhism very interesting because he could encounter it monk to monk. He could meet it in other monastics like himself, although in the Buddhist tradition. And remember the period is post–Vatican II, where there was the great revamping of monasticism in the Christian West, so it was a timely encounter in that regard.

Merton with other conference attendees not long before his death in Bangkok in 1968.

In the last letters that Merton sent back from Asia in 1968, just a matter of days before he died, he explicitly talks about the fact that he continued to be a Christian and he saw himself as such. Harold Talbott, the American who was with him when he met His Holiness the Dalai Lama, was quite firm about the fact that Merton would have remained in the church. He wasn't on the verge of shifting from the church to the Sangha, if I can put it in those terms.

Elena Malits: I think there's a very interesting thing that Merton says in the closing of *Zen and the Birds of Appetite*. He talks about how he and D. T. Suzuki had started out hoping to discover what Christianity and Buddhism had in common, what the similarities were. At the end he has a postscript in which he says, "That is a project that doesn't get you anywhere. What I learned from these years of trying to understand what Buddhism, or Zen in particular, and Christianity have in common is not to look at the particular beliefs, but to try to get at the underlying experience. And that's the hardest thing in the world to talk about. But at least you can know that there are other people, who on a different way, by a different path, have come to know something of the divine that you have come to know." Now I think that's an important thing for Merton to have said.

No Catholic scholar in the 1960s was writing about the great religious traditions of the East. Merton predated Vatican II in opening the way to the now common statement that God reveals himself in some way that we can't define in all of these traditions. But Merton was actively involved and believed it before anybody else was talking about it. I think that's one of those things where you can see how ahead of his time Merton was, and yet he would not have said "I'm a pioneer," but "I'm just going where I'm being led, step by step."

Paul Quenon: In his teaching and his spiritual direction he took a pretty objective approach to things. He wasn't just promoting his own interests. He was giving you what he thought would be best for your monastic life and what was the baggage of the tradition. Not baggage in a bad sense, but the richness, the wealth of the tradition. He had an interest in Buddhism, but he didn't push that. I think he only mentioned it two or three times in the two years that I had him as a teacher. Now if you would go to him with your interest in Zen, he might answer questions about that, but in his classes it didn't come up, perhaps a passing reference or something like that. So it didn't become an issue in the monastery, because he didn't really go that public about it.

I went to him once. I kept hearing this word "Zen" and so I said, "Well, what exactly is Zen?" Well, he thought that was the funniest question, you know. "What's the essence of Zen?" Well you're not dealing with essences when it comes to Zen. So he told me, "Well, go see Fr. Augustine about it"' He took a book and was about to hit me over the head. "That's the essence of Zen." He wouldn't give me a straight answer because you don't get straight answers in Zen. It took me another three years to find that out.

Jonathan Montaldo: One of Merton's implicit agendas in going to Asia was to meet and converse with Buddhist monks and lay practitioners of serious meditation. He wanted to meet people who were deep into Buddhist meditation so he could bring that back to his monastery, but first he had to get it himself. Remember, Merton didn't have any spiritual directors. He complained about it in his journals. So Merton was going to Asia to find spiritual directors who might help him achieve a breakthrough into a deeper mode of consciousness.

In 1968 Merton is not trying to figure out how he can become more socially active. Merton is looking for more and more solitude. That's instructive to realize. This is where his head always was in the monastic life. He's looking for more solitude, for a deeper experience of prayer and meditation that would transform his consciousness. He was serious about that. He said in his journals, "I need something that I don't even know yet, something that I don't even know that I don't have." And that's what he was looking for on his Asian trip. He wasn't going to hit the streets. He wasn't going to get married. He was going to go into deeper meditation.

Maurice Flood: I don't think most people in the community knew he was going to Asia until the last minute. Maybe Dom James wanted it that way. I might be wrong on that. But you know, Fr. Flavian Burns was elected, I think, January 18, 1968, and of course Fr. Louis notified the community before the election that he wasn't available to be abbot of what he called "this doghouse." He never wanted to be abbot of anything. He just wanted to be a monk. He approached Fr. Flavian about going to Asia to meet other monks. I guess Fr. Flavian said, "Well, you're a mature monk. I'm not going to tell you what to do. You work with me and you choose what you think you should do in the present situation of monasticism by way of sharing yourself with other monks, with other religious centers." I think that's the way it worked out, but most people didn't know this trip was really evolving until Merton was almost ready to leave.

Jonathan Montaldo: Dom Jean Leclercq, a Benedictine scholar of St. Bernard's writing and of medieval monasticism, invited Merton to address a meeting of monks of the East and West in Bangkok, Thailand. With Dom Flavian Burns's permission Merton accepted the invitation, not just to meet Buddhist laymen and monks but also to visit Cistercian monasteries in Asia. His itinerary definitely included a Cistercian monastery in Indonesia. He did have plans to visit Europe. A professor of Islamic Studies told a friend of mine that Merton was coming to visit him in Egypt after leaving Asia. It appears that Merton intended to take a "slow boat" to many ports of call before returning to Gethsemani.

Merton's journals during his Asian trip, published posthumously, reveal all of Merton's tourist interests. There is a moment in those journals that has become very significant for Merton's readers. Merton is in Ceylon at Polonnaruwa. He visits a temple area and encounters huge Buddhist sculptures. The one in repose is the Buddha himself as he lay dying. A standing figure is Ananda, the Buddha's disciple. Merton has a wonderful passage about the effect these sculptures had on him. He writes that his Asian journey had finally become clear, that he had found what he was looking for. "I have seen beyond the shadow and disguise," he wrote. But my sense of this is that he is acknowledging that he has finally seen beyond the shadow and disguise of Asia, beyond all its Westernization and Indian English kitsch, like Indians dressed in kilts and the legacy of the Raj. It's not that he is seeing beyond the shadow and disguise of life, in my reading, but that he had finally seen emanating from these sculptures the Asia he had come to encounter. It's a very moving passage that has heightened meaning because he is dead in a matter of days.

Some readers interpret this moment with the Buddhist sculptures as Merton's most important epiphany into what life is all about. Now he can go and die, they interpret it, since he is in some sense finally realized. But to my mind this is yet another event, like 4th and Walnut, and like his becoming an American citizen, that are links in a chain of important experiences transformed by his literary and artistic sensibilities into literature. Had Merton lived beyond Bangkok, he would probably have recorded more epiphanies as he went on. Possibly in Egypt in front of the pyramids?

Paul Pearson: The biggest misperception is shown in the question that I get asked almost by every group with whom I teach or work, "Was Merton about to leave the church and become a Buddhist at the end of his life?" One gets the impression from the Catholic bishops, having omitted him from the catechism for young adults recently, that certainly more conservative elements within the church thought that was the case. But for anybody who really takes the time to understand Merton, or to read in any depth about him, that would have been the last thing on his mind. If you look at the very last entry in his personal journal just two days before his death, he's going off to celebrate Mass. He's having lunch with the apostolic delegate in Bangkok. As he's traveling in Asia, he's very much continuing his own monastic tradition, celebrating Mass, saying the Divine Office, and maintaining his own daily personal devotions. He has his rosary with him. He's even carrying some relics of saints that have been sent to him over the years and an icon of the Blessed Virgin Mary with the infant Jesus.

When Merton meets with the Dalai Lama, just look at what the Dalai Lama says about Merton, that Merton was the first person who introduced him to the real meaning of the word Christian. You know Merton isn't going to the Dalai Lama and saying, "Can I become a Buddhist monk?" They're dialoging, but from the depths of their own tradition. Merton's dialogue with Buddhism, with other faiths, isn't any wishy-washy new age kind of thing, pulling bits from lots of different faiths to make some new faith. When he dialogues with other faiths it's from the depths of his own tradition, and that's true dialogue, I think.

Death

Merton goes to Asia and suddenly there is word that he has died. His death happens just that abruptly in Soul Searching. *I hope to jar the viewer much like his community, circle of friends, and readers must have been jarred when the news came that this vital force of life had been extinguished. There was no preparation for it. Some still seem to have not gotten over the trauma. His good friend, the poet Ron Seitz, describes the loss of Merton as creating an unfillable hole in his life. Seitz said another Merton friend, Dan Walsh, had told him in the aftermath he felt like he was split in half and that half of him was gone.*

What struck me most in discussing his death was the reaction of his Trappist brothers that I interviewed. They grieved their Fr. Louis, but their unsentimental view of death is challenging and as countercultural as their lifestyle.

Maurice Flood: It was at the end of the noon meal [at Gethsemani], after the reader had finished the reading and we were ready to get up

The Dalai Lama and Abbot Timothy Kelly at Thomas Merton's grave.

and do the dishes, Fr. Flavian [the abbot] came over to the podium where the monk read for the week and said, "I have some bad news. Father Louis is dead." And it was a week later that the body was returned for the funeral mass and burial.

Of course I was shocked when Merton's death was announced, but I don't think I thought it was bad news. Maybe the way it happened was rather abrupt, but here is somebody that's arrived at the place where he came to seek in the first place. So if it was by electrocution, it was kind of a rough way to go, but I think, great. When it comes to the end, well, that's the beginning. You're graduating. It's the big day! So if it comes sooner or later, you welcome it.

Paul Quenon: Well, when Merton died it was the most joyful experience in my life because it was seeing him come to term, you know. He had reached the goal. He became somebody more immediate to me than he ever was before. I could access him in a way that I couldn't before, through prayer and intercession. Of course I was in the refectory when Fr. Flavian came to the microphone. The abbot doesn't do that unless there's something really special. And then he announced that we had received news that there had been an accident and that Fr. Louis had died. He didn't know what the accident was. Immediately I went to church because I remember him telling me, "When I die, you guys say lots of *De Profundis*'s for me," which is the penitential psalm for those who have died. So I went to church and I said the seven penitential psalms like I'd never said them before or since perhaps.

Then I left church and walked down the cloister. You just had a sense that everything had stopped. Like there was a suspension in time. Same sort of feeling that you had after Kennedy was shot. I walked into the scriptorium and there's this great whoosh of steam coming out of the boiler. It would release now and then. But just as I walked in there was a great whoosh, like the spirit being released symbolized by this steam that was going out. When Jesus died on the cross he gave up the spirit. For a whole week, I think, there was that sense of time standing still, until his corpse came. It took a long time. I think it was almost a week and it got kind of heavy since it did take that long. It's nice to get people buried promptly the way we usually do.

I think one of the best things I heard was the story about when Dom Jean LeClercq, the Benedictine and medieval scholar, was given the news at the conference—Dom Jean was attending, too— that Fr. Louis had just died. He said, "*C'est magnifique!*" "That's great, magnificent!" I think that really puts the finger on my feeling. But of course it left a big hole in the world nobody else can fill. On the other hand, when a great tree falls the little trees can get more sunlight and spring up on their own. It's not always healthy to be overshadowed. On the other hand, life is much more interesting when you've got somebody special around like that.

Anthony Padovano: Certainly the story of Merton's death is very straightforward. He was in Bangkok. He was at a meeting of contemplatives, both Buddhist and Christian. He touched a fan after a bath in the afternoon. He was scheduled to have a question and answer period, deriving from his lecture earlier that morning, after a lunch and siesta break. And then he was found dead. There have been many theories about that and I tend to discount all of them. I don't think it was a conspiracy. I don't think that Merton, no matter how prominent he was, was done in by the CIA. I think that's a little bit bizarre. He was not so crucial to the Vietnam protest movement that it couldn't have gone on quite well without him. At that point that movement had taken off with its own dynamic. And the theory that he committed suicide doesn't make any sense to me.

I did ask the monks at Gethsemani, Patrick Hart his secretary most prominently, about what they thought of his death. Did conspiracy or a suicide theory seem plausible? Hart said, "Most of us are amazed that he didn't kill himself in the hermitage. He was unbelievably klutzy. He never learned how to drive a car. We kept expecting he was going to be found dead electrocuting himself in the hermitage. No, no, no. This fits

in with Merton." I am prepared to believe that. So it's a very strange oc-
currence, but I think it was what we have been told it was.

Paul Elie: It seems pretty clear that Merton's death allowed us to project
our own image of him onto him in the years since his death, allowed
people to claim Merton for this or that cause or movement or project,
to imagine what Merton would have thought, to purport to say what he
would have said. There's been a lot of misunderstanding as a result of
all that. What his death really points to, if you ask me, is the literal loss
of one of the great and holy figures of the church in this country for
twenty-five or thirty years. Merton died at age fifty-three. A priest of
fifty-three at this time in the life of the church is still a young priest. He
was five years older than John Paul II. He was close in age to Czeslaw
Milosz, the poet who died not too long ago. When one thinks of how
much happened for Catholics in this country in the time since Merton's
death, and what it would have meant for someone of that integrity and
wisdom to have been around, it boggles the mind. The 1970s: the free-
form liturgies, the struggle for the church to find its place in the world,
all sorts of searchings about the priesthood, getting together with other
religions, the election of John Paul II, the end of communism, the
church's involvement in the struggles of Central America, the rise and
demise of liberation theology, the struggles of women in the church and
on and on. Imagine if Merton could have been around, of great age but
undiminished, with things to tell us about all these concerns. I think the
life of the church in this country would have been strikingly different
had he lived.

Colman McCarthy: I've often wondered what would Thomas Merton
have been at eighty years old. I remember Andrew Young once said that
it was almost a blessing that King didn't live beyond his forties, because
he was still vibrant. His message was pure. He said, "My God, if King
ever lived to be eighty years old, he'd be so mellow by now." The same
with Merton, how would he have gone on? He died at fifty-three, just a

young fellow really. So that's something we'll never know, but one of the great ironies was that, when he was killed, he was flown home in a casket by an airplane that stopped in Saigon to pick up the bodies of American soldiers killed in the Vietnam War, and there was Merton who was bitterly opposed to the Vietnam War being flown home on an Air Force jet packed with caskets of American soldiers. The little ironies.

I wasn't aware of Merton when he died in 1968 so his passing had little impact on me, at least of which I was aware. I probably thought most about his death when I passed him chronologically. Initially I allowed it to be negative. "You're fifty-four years old; look what Merton had accomplished and he died at fifty-three." Fortunately this abuse couldn't last too long before collapsing under the absurdity of comparing lives. Yet, the reality was that I had—and still do—looked to him as the master, the pathfinder or "explorer," as Elena Malits would call him. Now I was entering years and hopefully decades of life which he had not experienced, at least in a physical sense. I was on my own, but at least he had left much with which to navigate.

Anthony Padovano: Merton died a very sudden death and I don't want to try in a Panglossian fashion to say it was the right moment and everything worked out fine and that's just as it should have been. But there do seem to be some elements of that there. Certainly his dying in the East, at a time when he was at a contemplative retreat with Buddhists, gives a sense of comprehensiveness to his life. It's a very powerful symbol. One can even say that maybe just about all that Merton had to tell us was said. That's difficult to say because he was a creative person and he may have gone in many different directions, but when I read his work, I don't read it in terms of the fact that there are unfinished themes that I wish he had been alive to complete. So I think there was a certain aptness about his death, although that's not what we would have chosen. Certainly his dying when he did and in those circumstances helped him make his death a kind of a metaphor and a symbol, dying trying to bring East and West together. I do think that there was something extremely fitting, more so than if he had died of a heart attack at Gethsemani in the hermitage, let us say, or died as a very old man who may have already said many of the things that he should have or would have developed. So I see his death as fitting, if you will.

Richard Sisto [describing the memorial service that took place in Louisville's Cathedral of the Assumption, after the funeral at Gethsemani]: The big church in Louisville was packed. Standing room only for Thomas Merton because even in those days he was very well known, the most well-known figure in our area, in Louisville. What a beautiful thing that was for us, because he wasn't even a Louisvillian. He wasn't even American, for that matter. They embraced him, and it was a beautiful Mass. I remember it was Fr. Flavian, the abbot of Gethsemani, who came in for the Mass. He was a very austere-looking man. He was also the abbot that gave Merton permission to do the Asian trip. He was certainly very quiet, but I knew him and he was by nature a quiet man. I remember I played a Miles Davis piece, a Miles Davis and Bill Evans piece. Merton loved, you know, that genre of jazz. There was a lot of music, people were all contributing, and it was a very soulful day.

Christine Bochen: We struggle don't we, on this side, in all of life? I don't think we ever get to the point of having arrived, if you will. You know, Merton was on the journey, he was living the journey. The endpoint of that journey was a new life, and a new life in God.

Part 4

Points West . . . and East

Merton's Legacy

As I began reviewing the "Merton choir" interviews for this book, I could see that there was one question I asked every person. What is Merton's legacy? Was he simply a gifted writer of his time or did his thought, work, and life example still have power today . . . and will it tomorrow?

Lawrence Cunningham: Thomas Merton was a Catholic monk, but to say only that he was a Catholic monk is to shrink what he was and what he meant to people. He was a great spiritual writer. He was a poet. He was a literary critic. He was a social critic and a writer of autobiographical reflections. He has been dead since 1968 and yet most of his books are still in print. Many of the people that find him a compelling figure are not people who would gravitate toward the writing of a Catholic monk. One of the reasons why Merton is so compelling a figure today is that he managed to write about very deep spiritual things, very deep convictions about the reality of God, without sounding particularly pious. He did not use the language of traditional piety. He spoke with the voice of a poet and he spoke out of deep experiences in his own life.

I think that Thomas Merton could easily be called the greatest spiritual writer and spiritual master of the twentieth century in English speaking America. There is no other person who has such a profound influence on those writing on spiritual topics, not only on Catholics but non-Catholics, as Merton has. The only contender would be the enormous popularity of C. S. Lewis. I think that they are very different

A view from near Christ in the Desert monastery in New Mexico. Photo taken by Thomas Merton.

kinds of persons who led very different kinds of lives. They both were greatly shaped by the English literary tradition, both of them were excellent writers, and both of them wrote out of very deep experience.

I borrowed the term "spiritual master" for Merton from an interview that I saw with Abbot Flavian Burns who said, "I have always regarded him as my spiritual master." He understood the term, as I do, in the original meaning of the word "master" and that is someone who's a teacher, not someone who masters over somebody else. So that the medieval teacher was a *magister*, and he was qualified by receiving the master of arts. And so I think of Merton as a spiritual master in the sense that he's a great spiritual teacher.

I don't think I could single out any single greatest contribution of Merton's. If you were to ask me what books are going to endure, say fifty years from now, I think I would name, first of all, *New Seeds of Contemplation*. It's a very idiosyncratic book in a way, but I think it's a profound book. I think in the American literary scene *The Seven Storey Mountain* is going to be known as a spiritual autobiography. I would think that *Thoughts in Solitude* is going to last. I think it's going to be his spiritual writings which are going to perdure over time. As a person, I think he serves as a model or a paradigm. We can't all obviously be Trappist monks, but he was a person who encountered the modern world, loved what was good about it, critiqued what was bad about it, responded to it from a deep sense of contemplative living. That's not a bad way to lead one's life.

William H. Shannon: There are people who really want to get Merton canonized as a saint. There's one person who has been writing to me wanting to get the cause of Merton's canonization put forward by somebody. I've written to those who write me of their desires that "I don't want to be involved in this in any way. I don't think that he should be canonized. I think he has already been canonized by people who really love him and appreciate what he did. I don't think that if he went through the canonization process that he would probably be able to pass it, because there are too many things in his life that would be questionable." I don't want him to be canonized anyway, because the canonizing would in a sense be putting him on a sort of a pedestal, and I want to see him as someone who's very much like all of us. If you want to call him a saint, that's fine, but what does it mean? He's a person who struggled to do the will of God, who realized his faults. His clay feet are there for all of us to see. He certainly would not want any kind of adulation given to him in the way of sainthood. He once had a letter from a young man who said that he wanted to become his disciple, and Merton wrote back and said, "Don't try to be. I don't have disciples. I don't want any disciples. Don't build your life on a mud pile like me. Be a disciple of Jesus Christ."

Lawrence Cunningham: I actually happen to be interested in the subject of hagiography, that is, writings about saints. There's one thing that's going to be very clear, and we know this already by the many biographies that have been written about Thomas Merton. You're not going to turn him into a saint according to the model of the kinds of saints that we were used to being told about when we were in high school or grammar school. He's not going to be a guy who is swooning in front of a statue of Our Lady uttering pieties. He makes fun of that kind of stuff actually in places.

Here's an interesting but very depressing fact. The American bishops are going to put out a new catechism based on the catechism of the Catholic Church. It's supposed to be for young people, and they're going to have a chapter, a biographical sketch of prominent American Catholics over the last couple of centuries, and they're not putting Thomas Merton in this book. I wrote to the man who's in charge of this and said, "This is outrageous." But they're fearful. They have a lot of little Nervous Nellies in the episcopacy, and they're worried that Merton was too interested in world religions, and so on and so forth. Now some of the people they are putting in are very good people, some of them saints. But no one's ever heard of them. No one's going to read them. Merton is unclassifiable. He's a kind of a dangerous thinker in a way and kind of a risk taker, and in this catechism, at least, he's paying the price for that.

Daniel Berrigan: When I was at Cornell University Thich Nhat Hanh came to speak, this would have been about 1967, and we became very good friends. He expressed his great desire to meet Merton and I set that meeting up although I couldn't go. Merton and he got on great too, as Merton testified, and one day down there at the monastery, I think it was at Merton's suggestion, they made a tape to record some greetings to me. So they did that and that was very beautiful. They each sang, Gregorian chant and Buddhist chant, and talked about those chants. They were getting on like a house on fire, and they sent me the tape, which was very precious. But I guess I bring up Nhat Hanh because I spent time in his Buddhist community, and in this very different world and setting he reminds me of Merton's integrity.

I think numbers of people are not going to be attracted to a monastic figure like him, but so what? Who else can I think of from the 1940s and 1950s who is still being read? Very, very few, and Merton is one of them. He is not just being read but also being published, and published about, and every aspect of his life and work taken up again and again. I think the legacy is sound and it's very nearly unique.

John Dear: Thomas Merton has emerged as perhaps the greatest monk in Christian history now. He is certainly on a level with St. Augustine and St. Thomas Aquinas in terms of his writing and his influence. He's reclaimed the best of Catholic spirituality and Christianity, the whole tradition of prayer and the desert and the Divine Office and the contemplative life. He influenced tens of thousands of people, among them a lot of men that I know in all the religious orders. I would ask them, "Why did you become a priest in the 1950s and 1960s?" And they would say, "Well, I read Thomas Merton's autobiography and it changed my life." A lot of other people had that experience too. What's so shocking is that Merton kept breaking new ground. He became the first Catholic priest in U.S. history to denounce nuclear weapons and war and racism, and he studied Mahatma Gandhi and the Chinese mystics and Zen Buddhism when most people had never heard of Zen or Buddhism. He was not only bringing cultures together, he was bringing the different religions together, and all the while going deep into the common ground of all of the religions, which is the wisdom of nonviolence. Recently one of the biggest Catholic theologians in the United States, David Tracy, said, "Where will the Church be two hundred years from now?" And he answered his own question without missing a beat: "We're all going to be trying to catch up to Thomas Merton. He's gone ahead of everybody." That's how significant a historical figure Merton now is, not just in the American Church, but maybe in the history of the church.

Kathleen Deignan: I'm not exactly sure who described Thomas Merton as a contemporary father of the church but what I'm discovering with Merton, the more that we recover and retrieve his own writings and see them published, is the breadth and the depth of his wisdom. I think we began to see the tip of the iceberg of his wisdom perhaps when he began to write in the late 1940s and continued through the late 1960s. Merton's powerful comprehension of this moment of time is a marvel, but as his correspondence, his diaries, and journal writings are published we begin to become aware of just how expansive and comprehensive his grasp of this boundary moment was, not just between centuries, the twentieth to the twenty-first, but between millennia. Merton, I think, profoundly comprehended the shifts, the tremendous shifts—we speak of paradigm shifts but they were tectonic shifts—that have been happening in our world and on our planet, for ever so many reasons.

So I find Merton, not so much that he is in any case a relic of the 1960s, rather I don't know that we have caught up with him yet. To me he's someone who moves ahead. He keeps expanding. The horizon keeps expanding as he recedes from us and we, I think, have to catch up to do the analysis and to do the work that he has set before us, if we're to comprehend this moment with its peril and its promise.

Robert Inchausti: Thomas Merton became the most famous monk in American history in a perverse fashion. He wanted to be a great writer, but then he decided that vocation was not something that he was called for; he was called to the monastery. After being there about five years he wrote an autobiography and that autobiography became an international best seller. Which was kind of a surprise to him and everybody else. This made him the most famous monk in American history, and after that he spent the rest of his life becoming a spokesman for the contemplative life and for the life of a monk living in a cloister.

He wasn't left wing and he wasn't really right ring, he was a contemplative culture critic, somebody writing from this sort of surprising and odd third point of view. After Merton's death his correspondence, his writings, became even more published, even more celebrated. In fact I think he's published more books after he died than he did when he was alive. So Merton's influence and fame have just sort of been growing, sort of exponentially, almost in spite of himself. It's a paradoxical thing for a monk to be world famous!

Merton was for us a late-twentieth-century Thoreau, in that he said, "Wait a minute, let's not give away the store to what is called progress. Is it really progress if we have to give up our own individuality and our own identities to achieve it?"

Merton, like Thoreau, is one of those mystery stories. I mean, he's laid the groundwork for nonviolent resistance to personal alienation and to appeals to our ego and appeals to ambitions that don't make our lives any better, don't make us any happier, don't make us any realer, and named them and called us on them, and then tried to live a life that was an alternative to that in every possible way. In those ways he becomes very interesting and instructive to those of us who can't go as far

Fr. Louis Merton died December 10, 1968.

as he did. One of the things I love about Merton is, he sort of made the decision, "OK, if I really believe that the news is nine-tenths nonevents, that the media is 100 percent manipulation, that economic ambition is an illusion, then I should drop out and live a life according to conscience with the monks." And he did it. He took that gamble. Now I'm sure when he originally joined the monastery, you know he was in his twenties, he couldn't have been sure that he hadn't misread everything. It had to be a leap of faith: "OK, I'll live it then!" Part of the thing that attracted him to the monks was that, while intellectuals and a lot of writers were social critics of the time, none of them followed through on the consequences of their logic: "If you don't believe in the system that is evolving, live an alternative life in order to demonstrate how one can still live and love life. Don't just take the benefits and harp about it." Part of our problems as non-Merton monks is that we've got one foot in and one foot out. Merton struggled very hard his whole life to try to make that honest commitment to a life lived in accordance with conscience as far as he could see it.

Merton's probably most famous for his writing, but he was also a photographer. Toward the end of his life he dabbled in photography and became more interested in photography as a way of articulating the silence. One of his interesting critiques, as a contemplative, was that the modern world was driving away silence. Everywhere there is noise. Now if he had seen today, where people walk down the streets with earplugs, plugging music into their heads or, you know, cell phones, he would sort of realize that silence was rapidly being emptied from our existence. Photography seemed to him a kind of an antidote to the noisiness of the world.

One of the coincidences of history that I pointed out in my book, *Thomas Merton's American Prophecy*, is the fact that Norman Mailer and Merton both wrote their first and major works in 1948. So Norman Mailer wrote *The Naked and the Dead* and Merton wrote *The Seven Storey Mountain*. Their careers were kind of like antithetical trajectories, where one decided to empty the ego and enter into pure obedience and to try to find reality that way. The other decided to strengthen the ego and enter into combat with the technological world, try to become a mayor and get on television, and sort of fight the good fight, and be the American existential hero that was defending the individual sensibility against the mega-corps or the new big institutions that were going to define all our lives for us.

Merton knew that being a human being he participated in a kind of fiction, a kind of false self. In fact he has one prayer where he says, "Lord let me always remember that I'm a liar and a deceiver, but that there's a part of me that always exists in you that transcends this and keeps me real." That is sort of like the opposite of Mailer's approach, which was to try to figure out the dynamics of this in worldly terms and beat the world at its own game. Merton's sense was that we need a psychology of the conscience or a spirituality of conscience that sees through our own personal falseness.

Now for me that is really unique and powerful in Merton. I think it defines his vocation as a writer in a way that makes him unique in later-twentieth-century writers. There are writers that deal with questions of identity and questions of the spirit, but nobody deals with our propensity to fool ourselves and to lie to ourselves. In fact one of his definitions of contemplation is, "Just stop lying to yourself for twenty minutes. Just stop! Stop thinking and lying to yourself for twenty minutes and see what happens." And that's what contemplation and meditation was for Merton, and that's what prayer is, you just say, "OK, what's reality? That's all I want. I don't want happiness, success, all these illusory things I think I need."

That's what I find in Merton that I would like every writer in America to be doing, tell us the story of their conscience, of seeing through their acts, rather than perpetuating upon me another performance, another virtuoso fake self that I'm somehow supposed to admire because it's brighter or more successful or it's prettier than somebody else's reality. I think we've seen through that. We don't need that. Nobody's interested in that anymore. That's why the media has become so boring. That's why these reality TV shows are just people praying that something true will come through. You know, "Maybe we'll catch somebody off-guard and they won't pretend." But we all know they're pretending the whole time and it's sort of like a melodrama of falseness that we're watching.

Coleman McCarthy: Merton was one of the first people to really bring the mystical life to a larger audience, a life of prayer, a life of sacrifice, and write about it in a way that people could say, "Yeah, I've always thought that myself, and now, what he says has confirmed my own ideas of what it's about." Merton was a clarifier of something that to most people was very foreign.

Merton is a gourmet item, as against other spiritual writers, because he was living the life that he was writing about. So there's a certain appeal to that: he was authentic, he was one of us looking for the answers, too. He gave us his ideas. You could say they were his guesses about what life means, about whether there's a God, whether there's a purpose beyond just our daily needs. People are always hounded by these questions. As long as those questions keep being asked, I think he'll probably be around, he'll be read. His other writings probably won't last as long, I don't think. We've had many great antiwar writers. We've had a lot of social justice people out there, but we haven't had the spirituality people, as Merton was.

I think he's a Western mind playing to Western thinkers and Western activists. I mean, very few people are global. I'm not trying to put him down, but he will always be an American. Gandhi's international in a way that Merton will never be, but even there, Gandhi in India is looked on as kind of a relic, someone of a distant time.

Michael Mott: He was a witness to his own times. He was somebody who pointed out the moral evils of his own time and who became remarkably brave. He does not start off brave. I won't say he was a coward, but he sure didn't have any reputation for courage. But in the '60s he's brave. And you need to be brave to be a prophet. His writing becomes very brave. His writing also becomes very acerbic. Courage, yes, he's got courage.

Anthony Padovano: Deep in our souls most of us feel a tug in the direction of God and the spiritual life. We're not quite sure if we're always helped by a particular religion. I think most people have respect for religion, but they're not certain that they want to be confined within those boundaries if those boundaries are too tight. Merton showed that you could find God in the spiritual life on a wide-ranging journey that can take you from Buddhism to Hinduism to Christianity to Judaism, and the real North Star leading you was God, this incredible need to touch God and experience God. Even though he was in such a rigid institution, the Cistercian community, Merton was less an institutional person and more someone who was hungry for God, yearning for God, sensitive for God.

Martin Marty: In 1967 the American Academy of Arts and Sciences got together a group of twenty young theologians and scholars to talk about religion. We talked about the Vatican Council. We talked about the death of God theology. We talked about the civil rights movement. And they had three secular scholars in there who said it's really interesting, at the end of this, that none of you, even for a second, talked about what most people think religion's about. Nobody mentioned prayer, or meditation, or spirituality, or whatever. So they assigned me the task, and I wrote an article called "The Search for a Spiritual Style in Secular America." I have to agree that the word "spiritual" wasn't used the way it is a half century later. It was very rare, but I pointed to a few places: Teilhard de Chardin, the Jesuit paleontologist, who was reinventing a Christian way of looking at evolution; Pope John XXIII had written *Journal of the Soul*; Martin Buber and Abraham Joshua Heschel were speaking inside Judaism; and among them all there was no more eloquent voice than Thomas Merton's. I would say for Catholicism in that period and subsequently, I'd rank his name with Dorothy Day.

When I am with people who remember the twentieth century, and I ask them to make their list of who are the people that they think will be remembered for these kinds of things a century from now, you'll get names like Albert Schweitzer, Gandhi, Martin Luther King Jr., Martin Buber, figures like that. And in all of that I would think many of them would put Merton. If there was one distinctive stamp they all had, it is that they were deeply rooted in a tradition but could reach to another. I saw a photo taken of a rice bowl, a loin cloth, a pair of spectacles, and a holy book. You'd look at that and say Gandhi, but Gandhi loved Jesus. Martin Luther King Jr. needed more nonviolence than he could get in Christian tradition. He needed Gandhi's *satyagraha*. I think that Merton is probably the prime bridger of these worlds, through his devotional writings, his prophetic writings, and his almost mystical writings.

Huston Smith: There is a saying, "beauty is in the eye of the beholder." Well prophets are in the eye of the beholder. I'm not sure that even I have associated that label with Merton, and I think he thanks me for that. I think of him as a holy man who did so much, partly through his writing, partly through his openness to other religions, and most of all through the example of the life that he lived.

Soul Searching at Gethsemani

As I thought about what Merton's legacy might be for me personally, my mind went back to the "monk's matinee" I played at the Abbey of Gethsemani soon after Soul Searching *was completed. I was arranging screenings for the program around the country when I received a message that Abbot Damien Thompson wanted me to do a showing for the community at Gethsemani. I was delighted to receive the invitation. In recent years while making films at the abbey, I had developed warm friendships with many of the brothers. Despite countless trips to the monastery I always looked for excuses to make the familiar trek to the place that has meant so much to me through the years. However as the day of the abbey premiere drew near, I found I was also more nervous than I would be for an ordinary showing. There would be no audience who would know more about my subject matter than this one and, more importantly, none that I wanted more to approve of the program.*

The day of the showing was a typical Kentucky winter day, gray with an icy mix of rain and sleet. Low-hanging clouds almost obscured the knoblike hills surrounding Gethsemani. I always wondered at how Merton, writing about the weather in his journals, could find vibrant life in such seemingly dull winter landscapes. Then I took the time to look.

Though Merton died in 1968, his enduring and some would say growing fame has kept the abbey a must-stop for spiritual seekers over the years. A claim can be made that it's the most famous monastery in America. This is a mixed blessing for the community who lives there. It's good for their "industry" of spiritual retreats and sale of food products but often proves a distraction from the vowed purpose of their lives—seeking union with God.

There are more than fifty men living in the community now. The median age is somewhere in the mid-seventies. The biggest surge in membership came in the late 1940s, a response to world conditions and Merton's writing. Men are still coming to Gethsemani today, but the numbers are fewer and now they tend to be middle-aged rather than fresh out of high school.

As I was completing my work on Soul Searching *one of the older monks asked me in a sincere, simple way if I would now be joining the community. I was surprised and tried to make light of the straightforward question, replying that I didn't think my wife would approve. I think it was a sign I'd been spending too much time there, but nonetheless I was flattered he considered me a candidate.*

Turning into the abbey entrance road a slick patch caused me to briefly skid sideways toward the wrought-iron gate that keeps unwanted visitors away from the cloistered area of the monastery. Literally or figuratively this is how I always seemed to arrive for visits. As always the same admonition applied—slow down.

The program showing was scheduled for 4 o'clock on a Sunday afternoon. Attendance was optional. Sunday afternoon is generally a free time for the monks. If I've learned anything in my time at Gethsemani, it's that though they live communally these men are individualistic in their interests. Free time might be given to any number of activities including pottery, photography, weaving, making rosaries, reading, writing letters, walks in the woods, visits from family, or a meridienne *(a great monastic euphemism for what I would call a nap).*

The audience numbered about twenty, which was about what I expected. Aside from the just-mentioned activities, I knew that some of the monks were ambivalent about their famous Brother Louis. Some are irritated by the crush of Merton admirers that can fill the monastery for certain occasions. Some quite rightly think there is a lot more to Gethsemani than the echoes of Thomas Merton. Others are more conservative, both in their politics and spiritual observances. Still others don't think about Merton much one way or the other. It has been four decades since he lived there.

The showing was in the chapter room, where the monks meet to discuss community affairs. It's a long room, probably one hundred feet, and relatively narrow, maybe twenty feet across. Its look is much like the rest of the monastery, suitably Spartan in décor and furnishings. The floor is terrazzo. The brick walls are bronze colored. There are no decorations, unless you count the felt banner decrying the death penalty that hangs on the wall. Two rows of wooden benches line each side of the room. In meetings the brothers sit on the benches, facing each other much as they do in choir. The abbot sits at one end of the room. He has an oversized wooden, throne-like chair. A large, stone crucifix hangs on the wall above his chair. It was a setting that could have been found in the fifteenth century except for my video projector and speakers.

The brothers provided the screen and it dropped from the ceiling. So much for the fifteenth century. I knew mine was not the only matinee that had been shown there. The community enjoys occasional screenings of films, usually consisting of spiritual fare. I do remember, however, one July 4th they were showing The Patriot, *Mel Gibson's recreation of Revolutionary War days. Walking down the cloister hallway that day I heard gunfire and the boom of cannons coming from the room. It was a little disconcerting in this house of prayer. Then again many of these men are veterans of World War II, so it wouldn't be the first time they had seen warfare. Though the austere life of a Trappist monk has softened somewhat over the years, most people still have a hard time picturing one going to a movie. It happens though. When* The Passion of the Christ *first came out, nearly the entire community was bussed into the local multiplex for a private showing.*

I gave brief remarks before the program began. I thanked them for the hospitality they had extended to me over some thirty years of visits. I recounted that I had first come there that long ago wanting to see where Merton had lived. I shared my story about reading The Seven Storey Mountain *and how it took me four tries to get through it because it was "too churchy." Polite chuckles. True to their vow of hospitality, they are almost always unfailingly polite. I was still nervous when the show began.*

I've shared Soul Searching *with many different audiences, but never with men who were actually living the life I'm trying to describe or recreate. They not only knew the subject of my program, they were his students, worked with him, worshiped with him, and shared his hard path. I was concerned that I'd gotten the details right, that I focused on the right things, and that I hadn't done anything to offend or shock. Though Merton was utterly frank in his seven volumes of journals and they are available for all to read (and are in the guest house library at the monastery), I was concerned that my depiction of his struggles with the demands of the monastic life, his outspoken advocacy of what might be labeled "liberal causes," his ongoing tensions with his abbot, his interest in and openness to Asian spirituality, and then of course his late-in-life romantic relationship with a nurse, might rankle some of the more conservative brothers.*

For the most part they watched attentively. The archival photographs of Gethsemani in the 1940s evoked a few murmurs. In many ways it must have been like a home movie for some. There were a few slight smiles, knowing nods and chuckles when the issue of monastic obedience was examined. The segment they seemed to enjoy most was the recounting of the interaction between Merton and Abbot James Fox. I suspect each has had his own issues with an abbot, past or present. One viewer who seemed to be enjoying himself was Fr. Matthew Kelty, ninety-one at the time, born the same year as Merton. Father Matthew had been a student of Merton's and later briefly served as his confessor. Father Matthew is a very gifted writer in his own right and renowned for the wisdom imparted in his homilies. I was gratified he seemed to like the show.

There was polite applause afterward. One brother said he appreciated my bringing out Merton's social justice advocacy. Another asked whether the project itself was hard to do. Feeling a bit ridiculous talking to these men about hardship, I replied that the only difficult thing was trying to decide which aspects of this complex man I should try to focus on. Then bells began to ring and my audience filed out silently, heading for another worship service.

As is the case with most showings, I had very much wanted the approval of the audience. In their taciturn way I think I received it from these kind monks. At another showing my wife had asked me how I hoped the audience would respond and my answer had been that a simple parade on Main Street would do. Filmmakers can be a needy bunch. Now the brothers were marching off to Vespers and that was close enough to a parade for me. As with virtually every trip I had made to Gethsemani, I had been given a gift. This time it was a deeper sense of perspective about a project that had been nearly all-consuming. Be open to the experience, embrace what is worthwhile, and then move on.

Abbey of Gethsemani, 2007. This is the view Merton would've had as he walked from his hermitage to the monastery.

After showing Soul Searching *to the community at Gethsemani, I walked outside to visit Merton's gravesite before heading home. In the distance I could see the hillside where Merton's beloved hermitage was located. Crows cawed as if still saluting their old neighbor. He always said it sounded like they were cursing. The rain had stopped during the show and ice glinted on the cedars that border the monastic cemetery. I'm reminded of photographs I've seen of soldiers' graves in Normandy—row after row of white crosses. Each has a bronze marker bearing the name of the monk buried underneath. On this day, as is often the case, Merton's grave stood out. It was adorned by a wreath with lavender berries brought by an admirer. It was the only cross with a wreath. My guess is that Merton, the good Trappist, would be embarrassed for standing out from the rest of the community. Someone has hung a St. Christopher's medal from one arm of the cross on his grave. A dove medallion hung from the other arm, swaying in a chilling breeze. A stone Buddha, small and smiling, sat in perpetual lotus position at the base of the cross. After all these years Merton was still the destination of varied pilgrims—hospitable and defenseless. I can imagine him smiling, seeing that so many different people are still sifting through his spiritual journey and finding parts that aid their own. I smiled as I left, knowing it is what I also have done. I am grateful.*

Biographies

John Eudes Bamberger, OCSO, is abbot emeritus at Our Lady of Genesee Abbey in Piffard, New York. He began his monastic life at the Abbey of Gethsemani where he was taught by Thomas Merton and later collaborated with him on numerous monastery projects. He is the author of *Thomas Merton: Prophet of Renewal*.

Daniel Berrigan, SJ, is a poet, peace activist, and Roman Catholic priest. Father Berrigan and his brother Philip were for a time on the FBI Ten Most Wanted Fugitives list for committing acts of vandalism including destroying government property while protesting the Vietnam War. He now resides in New York City and continues to be active in social justice issues.

Christine Bochen is a professor of religious studies at Nazareth College in Rochester, New York. She is a founding member and past president of the International Thomas Merton Society. She has edited numerous volumes of Thomas Merton's writings including *The Essential Writings*.

James Conner, OCSO, is the former abbot of Our Lady of the Assumption Abbey in Ava, Missouri. He is now a monk of the Abbey of Gethsemani. He was taught by Thomas Merton and later assisted him as undermaster of novices. He is a past president of the International Thomas Merton Society.

Lawrence Cunningham is the Rev. John A. O'Brien Professor of Theology at Notre Dame University. The author or editor of twenty books, he writes regularly for journals both learned and pastoral. Twice honored by the university for his teaching, he also received a Presidential Award in 2001 for his service to the church and the academy.

John Dear, SJ, is a priest, peace activist, and retreat leader. He is the author or editor of twenty books on peace and nonviolence. After the September 11, 2001, attacks on the World Trade Center, he became one of the coordinators of the chaplains program at Ground Zero.

Kathleen Deignan, CND, is an educator, theologian, and composer. A sister of the Congregation of Notre Dame, she is a professor of Religious Studies at Iona College in New Rochelle, New York, where she founded and directs the Iona Spirituality Institute.

Paul Elie is a writer and editor. His book *The Life You Save May Be Your Own: An American Pilgrimage* received a 2004 National Book Critics Circle Award nomination. Since 1993 he has been an editor at Farrar, Straus and Giroux.

Maurice Flood, OCSO, a monk of Holy Cross Monastery in Berryville, Virginia, was a student of Thomas Merton's at Gethsemani. He serves as chaplain to the Cistercian community at the Redwoods Monastery in California.

Robert Inchausti is a professor of English at California Polytechnic State College. He is the author of four books and the editor of two anthologies of Thomas Merton's writings. His book *The Ignorant Perfection of Ordinary People* was nominated for a National Book Award.

Elena Malits, CSC, is a professor of religious studies at Saint Mary's College, Notre Dame, Indiana. She is the author of *The Solitary Explorer: Thomas Merton's Transforming Journey.*

Martin E. Marty is the Fairfax M. Cone Distinguished Service Professor Emeritus at the University of Chicago, where he taught chiefly in the Divinity School for thirty-five years. The Martin Marty Center has since been founded to promote "public religion" endeavors. He is the recipient of numerous honors, including the National Humanities Medal, the National Book Award, the Medal of the American Academy of Arts and Sciences, and the University of Chicago Alumni Medal.

Colman McCarthy is the founder and director of the Center for Teaching Peace in Washington DC. He wrote for the *Washington Post* for over twenty-five years and is on the adjunct faculty at American University, Georgetown University Law Center, the University of Maryland, and he teaches a daily class at Bethesda-Chevy Chase High School.

Jonathan Montaldo is the resident director of Bethany Spring, the Merton Institute Retreat Center one mile from the Abbey of Gethsemani. He is a former director of the Thomas Merton Center at Bellarmine University and a past president of the International Thomas Merton Society. He has edited several books on Merton, including the series Bridges to Contemplative Living with Thomas Merton.

Michael Mott is a novelist, poet, biographer, and editor born and educated in England. He has received awards and critical acclaim for his poetry and novels. His biography, *The Seven Mountains of Thomas Merton*, was nominated for a Pulitzer Prize and received a 1985 Christopher Award.

Anthony T. Padovano holds doctorates and professorships in theology and literature. He is the author of twenty-eight books including *The Human Journey*. He has been visiting professor at twenty-five American colleges and universities, lectures worldwide, and appears regularly in the media on both sides of the Atlantic.

Paul M. Pearson is director and archivist of the Thomas Merton Center at Bellarmine University, a past president of the International Thomas

Merton Society, and a founding member of the Thomas Merton Society in England and the British Isles. He is the editor of Thomas Merton's *Seeking Paradise: The Spirit of the Shakers.*

Paul Quenon, OCSO, is a monk of the Abbey of Gethsemani. He is a published poet, most recently of the volume *Monkswear*, and has been active in sharing the work of his former teacher Thomas Merton with the general public.

Rosemary Radford Ruether is the Carpenter Emerita Professor of Feminist Theology at the Pacific School of Religion and Graduate Theological Union in Berkeley, as well as the Georgia Harkness Emerita Professor of Applied Theology at Garrett Evangelical Theological Seminary. She is the author of many books, including *Women and Redemption.*

William H. Shannon is professor emeritus at Nazareth College in Rochester, New York. He is the founding president of the International Thomas Merton Society, and was the general editor of the Thomas Merton Letters and coauthor of *The Thomas Merton Encyclopedia.* He is author of the much-acclaimed biography of Merton, *Silent Lamp*, as well as a number of books on spirituality.

Richard Sisto is a musician and teacher of meditation who lives in Louisville, Kentucky. He has recorded numerous albums of jazz. He contributed original compositions for the documentary on Merton, *Soul Searching.* He visited and corresponded with Merton in the 1960s.

Huston Smith is internationally known and revered as the premier teacher of world religions and for his bestselling books *The World's Religions* and *Why Religion Matters.* He was the focus of a five-part PBS television series with Bill Moyers, and has taught at Washington University, the Massachusetts Institute of Technology, Syracuse University, and the University of California, Berkeley.

Bonnie B. Thurston is a Disciples of Christ minister and is a founding member of the International Thomas Merton Society and served as its third president. She is the author of eleven theological books, two volumes of poetry, and over one hundred articles, twenty of which are on Thomas Merton. She is the editor of *Thomas Merton and Buddhism*.

Monica Weis, SSJ, is a professor of English at Nazareth College in Rochester, New York, and is a past vice president of the International Thomas Merton Society. She is the author of *Landscapes of Paradise: Thomas Merton's Gethsemani*.

Photo Credits

Photo on page viii by John Lyons, used with permission of the Merton Legacy Trust and the Thomas Merton Center at Bellarmine University, Louisville, KY.

Photo on page 4 by Marcel Cabrera.

Photos on pages 14, 102, 111, 120 (bottom), 150, 189, 198, and 206 by Morgan Atkinson.

Photo on page 18 courtesy of Clare College Archives.

Photo on page 29 by George M. Aronson, courtesy of Corpus Christi Parish.

Photo on page 36 courtesy of Corpus Christi Parish.

Photos on page 44, 57, and 68 courtesy of Abbey of Gethsemani archives.

Photos on pages 52 and 168 used with permission of the Merton Legacy Trust and the Thomas Merton Center at Bellarmine University, Louisville, KY.

Photo on page 85 by John Howard Griffin, used with permission of the Merton Legacy Trust and the Thomas Merton Center at Bellarmine University, Louisville, KY.

Marcel Cabrera and Steve Staley were directors of photography for the documentary Soul Searching: The Journey of Thomas Merton. *Marcel (top) is shown by the shore near Bear Harbor, California, and Steve (bottom) is shown in New Mexico near Christ in the Desert monastery. Their vision brought light to the project.*

Photos on pages 94, 116, 128, and 182 by Thomas Merton, used with permission of the Merton Legacy Trust and the Thomas Merton Center at Bellarmine University, Louisville, KY.

Photos on page 120 (top) and 175 used with permission of the Thomas Merton Center at Bellarmine Univerity, Louisville, KY.

Photo on page 139 by Robert Lax, courtesy of Richard Sisto.

Acknowledgments

With gratitude to the people at the Merton Institute for Contemplative Living. Their encouragement made this book possible. Special thanks to Barbara L. Watts who spent countless hours transcribing the interviews.